Deschutes
Public Library

D1013077

C.1

DEAD ZONES

WHY EARTH'S WATERS ARE LOSING OXYGEN

CAROL HAND

TWENTY-FIRST CENTURY BOOKS / MINNEAPOLIS

Text copyright © 2016 by Lerner Publishing Group, Inc.

All rights reserved. International copyright secured. No part of this book may be reproduced, stored in a retrieval system, or transmitted in any form or by any means—electronic, mechanical, photocopying, recording, or otherwise—without the prior written permission of Lerner Publishing Group, Inc., except for the inclusion of brief quotations in an acknowledged review.

Twenty-First Century Books
A division of Lerner Publishing Group, Inc.
241 First Avenue North
Minneapolis, MN 55401 USA

Main body text set in Caecilia LT Std 9/15
Typeface provided by Adobe Systems.

For reading levels and more information, look up this title at www.lernerbooks.com.

Library of Congress Cataloging-in-Publication Data

Hand, Carol, 1945–
      Dead zones : why Earth's waters are losing oxygen / by Carol Hand.
      pages cm
    Audience: 12–18.
    Audience: Grades 9 to 12
    ISBN 978-1-4677-7573-1 (lb : alk. paper)
    ISBN 978-1-4677-9575-3 (EB pdf)
    1. Fish kills—Juvenile literature. 2. Fishes—Effect of water pollution on—Juvenile literature. 3. Anoxic zones—Juvenile literature. 4. Marine eutrophication—Juvenile literature. 5. Nutrient pollution of water—Juvenile literature. I. Title.
SH174.H36 2016
639.2—dc23   2014041304

Manufactured in the United States of America
1 – VP – 12/31/15

CONTENTS

1 DEATH IN THE DEPTHS

For two years, veteran fisher Mauricio Blanco worked off the Gulf Coast of Louisiana, but he caught almost no fish. He has since moved west to the tiny community of Port O'Connor, Texas. There he spends half the year—mid-May to mid-October—harvesting oysters from offshore reefs. He spends the other half of the year trawling for shrimp, which he sells to other fishers to use as bait. His catches are low, and fuel for his boat is expensive, but Blanco manages to make a living.

Others aren't so lucky. At one time in the late twentieth century, about three hundred fishing boats docked at Port O'Connor, but in 2014, only about ten boats docked there. Dirk Guidry of Chauvin, Louisiana, was once a shrimper, but to survive and remain in the area, he sold his boat and opened a pizza restaurant. Darren Martin still harvests shrimp, but he must go farther and farther from shore to find them, increasing his fuel and labor costs. "Unlike a farmer,

Fish killed by a dead zone cover a beach in Marina del Rey, California, in May 2014.

we can't see the crop," Martin says. "If you're used to going to a certain area [of the Gulf], and you go out and the dead zone is there, you're in trouble."

Why are some shrimpers and fishers going out of business? Why is the seafood catch declining? And what is this "dead zone" that shrimper Martin refers to?

The problem begins as many as 2,000 miles (3,219 kilometers) away, in the upper reaches of the Mississippi River. Corn farmers in Iowa, Illinois, and surrounding states feed their crops massive amounts of fertilizers containing nitrogen and phosphorus, which provide nutrients for the plants. As spring rains and water from irrigation systems wash over the fields, fertilizer runs off the land and enters streams, small rivers, and eventually the Mississippi. As it travels south to the Gulf of Mexico, the mighty river continues to pick up fertilizer runoff from farms and suburban lawns. Manure from animal feedlots also washes into the river. It too contains large amounts of nitrogen and phosphorus.

A midwestern farmer sprays fertilizer on a field of crops. Some of this fertilizer, which contains large amounts of nitrogen and phosphorus, will run off with rain or irrigation waters, ending up in streams, rivers, and eventually the Gulf of Mexico. There, the nitrogen and phosphorus will contribute to the growing Gulf dead zone.

When this nutrient-rich freshwater soup reaches the Gulf of Mexico, it provides food for tiny single-celled algae called phytoplankton. Nourished by nitrogen and phosphorus, phytoplankton populations bloom, or explode, in the Mississippi Delta, the area where the river meets the Gulf of Mexico. Zooplankton, tiny creatures that feed on phytoplankton, cannot eat or reproduce rapidly enough to control the algal growth. As algal blooms become too dense, the algae run out of nutrients, begin to die, and fall through the water toward the ocean floor. Bacteria then bloom as they break down the vast quantities of dead algae.

As bacteria decompose the dead algae, they consume most or all the oxygen from the water near the ocean floor, creating a dead zone below the surface. Dead zones seldom occur at the surface of a body of water. There, both photosynthesis (a process by which green plants use sunlight to make food while releasing oxygen) and wind and wave action constantly add oxygen to the surface water. In the depths, there are no processes to add oxygen. So when bacterial populations explode, they can quickly deplete the existing oxygen supply.

Dead zones (or hypoxic zones, as scientists call them) are regions of freshwater or salt water with low oxygen or no oxygen at all. They are found all over the world. Oxygen levels in dead zones are so low that few or no organisms can survive there. When a dead zone begins to form, fish and other swimming animals will leave the area. But without oxygen, bottom-dwellers such as crabs, clams, and worms will die of suffocation.

Warm water can't hold as much oxygen as cold water, so the dead zone in the Gulf of Mexico peaks in the heat of summer. It breaks up in late August or September, as temperatures begin to fall and as tropical storms stir up the water and replenish the oxygen at deeper levels. This cycle repeats itself every year.

FISH ON THE DECLINE

Just looking out over the Gulf of Mexico, it is difficult to see a dead zone. The surface looks normal. Sometimes fish are even visible near the surface. The dead zone is deeper. When researchers dive to the bottom to view the dead zone up close, they see no fish or other animals. They see only mats of white bacteria that one researcher has compared to snot. When healthy, the Gulf floor teems with many kinds of life, but in a dead zone, it is covered with grayish-black, foul-smelling goo.

Gulf shrimper Albert Darda Jr. describes shrimping in the dead zone. "We have video fish finders and [other] things on the boat that we use to locate the seafood," Darda says, "and these things just show the bottom completely blank." Darda sometimes searches for several days—twenty-four hours a day—before finding an area with shrimp.

When fish and shrimp leave dead zones, they do not return the following year, so shrimpers like Darda must find new fishing grounds. The loss of predictable fishing grounds results in lower catches and more work for less reward. Because of dead zones, many shrimpers and fishers have gone out of business. And as seafood becomes scarcer, it becomes more expensive. The high prices harm fish restaurants, food distributors, and other businesses that rely on selling affordable seafood.

Not all organisms die or leave when dead zones form. Some organisms survive in low-oxygen environments by limiting their energy use. According to Louisiana shrimper Lance Nacio, "In September and October, shrimp go dormant [a state similar to hibernation] to survive the dead zone." Other animals produce fewer eggs or none at all. Biologist Peter Thomas of the University of Texas Marine Science Institute in Port Aransas explains, "The way many of these marine organisms survive as a population is to have millions of eggs. But making millions of eggs is hugely energy dependent and so animals that face severe stress through things like hypoxia stop reproduction. . . . These fish think, if they survive till next year, they'll reproduce in another year. The problem is, the hypoxia occurs every year." Over time, fish populations decline.

"MAKING MILLIONS OF EGGS IS HUGELY ENERGY DEPENDENT AND SO ANIMALS THAT FACE SEVERE STRESS THROUGH THINGS LIKE HYPOXIA STOP REPRODUCTION."

PETER THOMAS, UNIVERSITY OF TEXAS MARINE SCIENCE INSTITUTE

According to marine scientists Robert Diaz and Rutger Rosenberg, dead zones have become a "key stressor on marine ecosystems." In the Chesapeake Bay in Maryland and Virginia, hypoxia causes harm all the way along the food chain. The damage starts with decreased reproduction of bottom-dwellers such as worms and clams. Fish that normally eat the bottom-dwellers have less food, which results in lower reproduction rates, which in turn yields lower catches for fishers. In addition, a bacterial disease called mycobacteriosis is increasing among striped bass, an important source of income for Chesapeake Bay fishers and seafood businesses. Scientists think the disease may be linked to oxygen depletion.

Chesapeake Bay loses about 5 percent of its food energy every year. That is, in dead zone areas, bottom-dwelling organisms such as

FISH ON THE BEACH

It's not always possible for fish and other swimming animals to escape dead zones. Sometimes, when oxygen loss is extremely rapid or animals have nowhere to go, dead zones kill large numbers of fish. Masses of dead fish quickly float to the surface or wash up on the nearest beach. The result can be tons of rotting animal flesh, a foul stench, and a massive cleanup for coastal residents. Such a fish kill, resulting from hot temperatures combined with an algal bloom, occurred in Marina del Rey, California, in May 2014.

In some places, the organisms do not die but try to swim away, and people welcome live seafood as it comes to shore. In Mobile Bay, Alabama, this sometimes occurs in late summer, when an underwater dead zone blows toward shore. Light winds push low-oxygen bottom water into the bay. Fish and shellfish swimming ahead of the water are trapped and wash up onshore. When locals see this incoming flood of seafood, they shout "Jubilee!" to spread the word. Everyone rushes out to gather blue crabs, eels, flounder, and other seafood while the organisms struggle helplessly in the surf.

---

clams and worms either have stunted growth or are prevented from reproducing. Fewer clams and worms mean less food energy available for their predators, such as fish. Northern Europe's Baltic Sea, which contains seven of the world's ten largest dead zones, has lost 30 percent of its food energy since its dead zones first started forming in the 1970s, and its fisheries have declined significantly. Diaz, of the College of William and Mary in Virginia, explains that enough food energy is lost to hypoxia in the Gulf of Mexico to feed 75 percent of Louisiana's average annual brown shrimp harvest. Lower reproduction of zooplankton and tiny fish results in lost food for shrimp. Fewer small animals on the ocean floor—such as worms, sea stars, and other crabs—means less food for crabs. Diaz asks, "If there was no hypoxia and there was that much more food, don't you think the shrimp and crabs would be happier? They would certainly be fatter."

DEAD ZONE DISASTER

Diaz remarks, "Dead zones were once rare. Now they're commonplace. There are more of them in more places." The Gulf of Mexico is a case in point. Until the 1950s, dead zones rarely formed in the Gulf. The US National Oceanic and Atmospheric Administration (NOAA) began noting recurring dead zones in the Gulf in 1972. In the twenty-first century, dead zones in the Gulf are a yearly occurrence. Although the sources of excess nutrients vary, similar dead zones are found in more than five hundred bodies of water around the world.

Many dead zones occur off the coasts of the developed, or industrialized, world, which includes the United States and the nations of Europe. In these nations, large farms use huge amounts of fertilizers. For example, every year, farmers in the United States apply 55 million tons (50 million metric tons) of synthetic (human-

Around the world, many cities let untreated sewage and other waste flow directly into the ocean. This picture shows a beach along Guanabara Bay in Rio de Janeiro, Brazil. Garbage litters the beach, and the water contains untreated waste. Heavy in nitrogen and phosphorus, such waste contributes to the growth of dead zones.

made) fertilizer to their fields. US farm animals produce 500 million tons (454 million metric tons) of manure per year. Much of this nutrient-rich manure is also used as fertilizer. Farmers spray it onto their fields to nourish their crops. But as with synthetic fertilizer, a lot of the manure runs off into lakes and rivers. Runoff from fertilizer-drenched lawns and golf courses also pours into bodies of water. In the United States and other industrialized nations, a majority of human and factory waste is removed from water at sewage treatment plants. However, in poor nations in Latin America, Africa, and Asia, communities often send untreated human sewage, wastewater, and industrial waste—containing large amounts of nitrogen and phosphorus—directly into rivers or the ocean. For

SOURCES OF EXCESS NUTRIENTS IN WATER BODIES

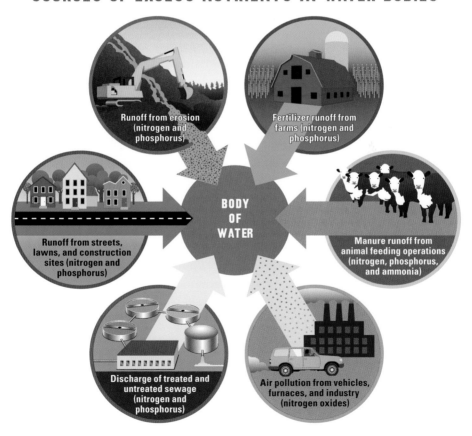

Runoff from erosion (nitrogen and phosphorus)

Fertilizer runoff from farms (nitrogen and phosphorus)

Runoff from streets, lawns, and construction sites (nitrogen and phosphorus)

BODY OF WATER

Manure runoff from animal feeding operations (nitrogen, phosphorus, and ammonia)

Discharge of treated and untreated sewage (nitrogen and phosphorus)

Air pollution from vehicles, furnaces, and industry (nitrogen oxides)

Cyanobacteria, which cause algal blooms and dead zones, have invaded many freshwater bodies. In this photograph, a fisherman in China's Anhui Province scoops up some of the bacterium-filled water.

example, São Paulo, Brazil, with a population of 18 million, treats only 10 percent of its sewage before discharging it into waterways.

Air pollution also contributes to dead zones. The burning of fossil fuels—coal, petroleum, and natural gas—puts excess nitrogen into the air. Rain and snow carry the nitrogen back to the land and water. Large industrialized nations such as the United States and China burn vast amounts of fossil fuels, adding to the dead zone problem in these places.

Oil spills at sea can make dead zones worse by coating the ocean surface, preventing oxygen from reaching deep water. The warmer temperatures brought by global climate change—caused by the burning of fossil fuels—can also exacerbate dead zones.

Dead zones also occur in many freshwater bodies around the world. Scientists report that in the United States, 31 percent of streams and lakes have excess levels of phosphorus, and 32 percent have excess nitrogen. In addition to causing dead zones, these elements can make the water unsafe to drink.

Aquaculture ponds, or fish farms, also contribute to dead zones. In these ponds, fish do not get their food from the wild. Instead, pond operators feed them large quantities of nitrogen-rich food. The fish use only about 20 percent of the food they receive for growth, part of the remainder is never eaten, and the fish excrete the rest. In other words, 80 percent of aquaculture food becomes pollution. Because the fish are contained in ponds, the pollution is very concentrated. At coastal fish farms, fish live in cages along the seacoast. Although their waste moves slowly toward the sea, most of it remains in shallow water, where it causes algal blooms and is eventually broken down by bacteria. This massive bacterial action quickly depletes the oxygen in the water.

The number of dead zones on Earth has doubled every decade since the 1960s. In 2013 dead zones covered more than 96,525 square miles (250,000 sq. km) of area in both freshwater bodies (rivers, ponds, and lakes) and saltwater bodies (oceans).

THE NUMBER OF DEAD ZONES ON EARTH HAS DOUBLED EVERY DECADE SINCE THE 1960S.

These dead zones profoundly affect the economy. In the United States, they cost the tourism industry more than $1 billion annually. No one wants to swim or boat in smelly, algae-filled waters. In addition, some algae produce toxins, causing fewer people to fish recreationally because they fear the fish may be contaminated. The fish and shellfish industries lose tens of millions of dollars yearly due to lower yields. Algal blooms also decrease property values and increase water treatment costs. Large-scale cleanup of water bodies can cost billions of dollars. In these ways, dead zones—even when they last for only part of each year—affect every aspect of ecosystems and societies.

2 OXYGEN FOR LIFE

lmost all living organisms—plants, animals, and microbes—require oxygen to survive. Land animals breathe in oxygen from the air. Aquatic animals take in dissolved oxygen (called DO by scientists) from the water. Without dissolved oxygen, our waters would have almost no life. They would certainly have no large swimming life.

Different types of aquatic organisms require different amounts of oxygen. Some fish species, such as trout, can survive only when DO levels are high. Other fish, such as carp and catfish, can survive with much lower levels. Zooplankton and many bottom-dwellers, such as worms and crabs, also survive with lower levels of dissolved oxygen. Because oxygen is vital to sea life, ecologists often use DO measurements as indicators of the health of an aquatic environment.

All aquatic organisms obtain oxygen from two sources. First, oxygen from the atmosphere dissolves into water. Wind and wave

The type of animals found at the bottom of a body of water depends on how much oxygen is present. Some animals can survive at low oxygen levels, and others need much more.

action speeds up this process. Second, oxygen is produced by photosynthesis, both on land and in water. In this process, green plants, algae, and a few types of bacteria make their own food from inorganic (nonliving) compounds. Using energy from the sun, they combine carbon dioxide and water to produce plant sugars. Photosynthesis releases oxygen as a by-product and provides plants with food in the form of sugar.

Oxygen is lost from water by respiration, a series of natural chemical reactions by which living organisms break down food to release energy. The food may be any type of organic matter, from living organisms to organic pollutants such as methane and other petroleum products. The two main types of respiration are aerobic respiration, which requires oxygen, and anaerobic respiration, which requires compounds besides oxygen, such as sulfates. Oxygen is also lost from water by chemical reactions, such as the decomposition of dead matter.

A few types of bacteria and other microbes are anaerobic. That is, they do not require oxygen to carry out respiration and obtain energy for life. Some of these organisms die in the presence of oxygen. Others can live without oxygen but use oxygen when it is available. All organisms, whether or not they can use oxygen, must still undergo respiration—that is, they must break down organic compounds to release energy. Many anaerobic bacteria use sulfates rather than oxygen for respiration. They release the smelly compound hydrogen sulfide as a waste product. If you drive past a swamp or marsh and get a whiff of something that smells like rotten eggs, you know that anaerobic respiration is happening.

DISSOLVED OXYGEN

The amount of oxygen dissolved in any body of water is much lower than its concentration in air. For example, Earth's atmosphere contains about 21 percent oxygen. But oxygen concentrations in healthy water are naturally low enough to be expressed not as percentages (parts per hundred) but as parts per million (ppm). For instance, 10 ppm equals ten molecules of oxygen for every one million molecules of water. (For comparison, 1 million molecules of air contain 210,000 molecules of oxygen.) At concentrations of 7 to 11 ppm oxygen, both cold- and warm-water fish can thrive. Warm-water fish can live at levels as low as 4 to 7 ppm. At levels of 2 to 4 ppm, only a few fish and insects will survive. Below 2 ppm, nearly all life requiring oxygen will die.

Ecologists define a dead zone to be any body of water with an oxygen concentration of 2 ppm or less. The US Environmental Protection Agency (EPA) has categorized the effects of low DO levels on aquatic organisms:

- At about 3 ppm, bottom fishes begin to leave the area and sensitive crab larvae (newly hatched, immature crabs) die.

- At 2.5 ppm, the larvae of less sensitive species, such as mud crabs and grass shrimp, begin to die, and crab growth is greatly limited.
- Below 2 ppm, juvenile fish and crustaceans (crabs, shrimp, and their relatives) that cannot leave the area will die.
- Below 1 ppm, all fish either leave the area or die. However, some clam species can survive at this level for weeks.

Sometimes dissolved oxygen is expressed as percent saturation. Complete, or 100 percent, saturation indicates that a water body holds as much oxygen as it can. This amount varies according to temperature, water pressure, and other factors. For example, cool water can hold more oxygen than warm water. Supersaturation occurs when, for a short time, the water holds more oxygen molecules than would be expected at that temperature or pressure. Supersaturation can occur on very sunny days when photosynthesis is high—that is, when plants are actively turning sunlight, water, and carbon dioxide into food and releasing oxygen as a by-product. Supersaturation may also occur when water is turbulent and a lot of oxygen is being mixed in from the air. Percent saturation can indicate the health of a body of water. Saturation levels of 80 to 100 percent or more (supersaturation) are excellent for animal health. Levels below 60 percent indicate oxygen deficiency and poor conditions for life.

DISSOLVED OXYGEN IN FRESHWATER

Oxygen concentrations in freshwater vary according to natural conditions, including water movement, temperature, time of day, time of year, water depth, and the number of plants growing in the water. Flowing water contains more oxygen than still water because motion causes oxygen to mix in from the air. Obstacles such as rocks

River water flowing over rocks contains more oxygen than still water. As the river churns and bubbles, oxygen from the air mixes in with the water.

in the water increase this mixing. A rapid mountain stream flowing over rocks contains more dissolved oxygen than a still lake or a broad river flowing smoothly toward the sea.

Water temperature also plays a role. Freshwater at 32°F (0°C) can hold up to 14.6 ppm of oxygen, but at 68°F (20°C), it can hold only 9.07 ppm. That's one reason why oxygen levels decrease, and dead zones are more likely to form, during warm summer months. However, oxygen can also be low in winter. When lakes and ponds freeze over, they become sealed environments. The top layer of ice prevents oxygen in the air from entering the water below. Near the end of winter, fish and other organisms trapped under the ice may run out of oxygen and die.

Oxygen concentrations in ponds and lakes fluctuate over a twenty-four-hour cycle. Photosynthesis can increase dissolved oxygen only during the day, not at night, since photosynthesis cannot take place without sunlight. Aerobic respiration—the process by which living things use oxygen to release energy—occurs both day and night. However, because there is no photosynthesis at night to release oxygen, oxygen levels decrease at night. Oxygen concentrations also vary according to depth. For instance, oxygen mixes in at the surface of a body of water due to wind and wave action but can reach near-zero levels near the bottom. Low levels also occur in sediments. Sediment-dwelling decomposers, mostly bacteria and fungi, consume the oxygen, which is not replaced by photosynthesis or through dissolving. A certain number of plants can increase the health of an aquatic ecosystem by adding oxygen through photosynthesis. But too many plants will overwhelm an ecosystem. As excess plants die, sink, and are broken down by bacteria, oxygen levels are depleted and dead zones form.

AS EXCESS PLANTS DIE, SINK, AND ARE BROKEN DOWN BY BACTERIA, OXYGEN LEVELS ARE DEPLETED AND DEAD ZONES FORM.

The water in deep lakes and ponds turns over in spring and fall, as water temperature changes at the surface. Spring and fall overturns are exactly what they sound like—warm water at the top sinks to the bottom, and cold bottom water rises to the top. During summer, water mixes less, remaining stratified, or layered, with warmer water at the top and cooler water at the bottom.

DISSOLVED OXYGEN IN OCEAN WATER

Oceanic dead zones occur in coastal bays, gulfs, and deltas. In these areas, water is shallow compared to the open ocean (which is an average of several miles deep) and productivity (the rate at which photosynthesizers produce new living matter) is high. As in freshwater, these environments show seasonal variations in dissolved oxygen. The lowest levels occur in late summer, when temperatures are highest. Hypoxia usually occurs in bottom sediments and the deepest water levels. In some dead zones, such as the Gulf of Mexico, hypoxia can extend up to 66 feet (20 meters) from the ocean floor. In some cases, it may occur throughout the water column—from the ocean floor all the way to the surface.

Salinity, or salt content, also strongly influences the amount of dissolved oxygen in seawater. The saltier the water is, the less oxygen it can hold. Water in the open ocean has a relatively constant salinity of 35 parts per thousand (ppt), or 3.5 percent, compared to almost no salt in freshwater. About 20 percent less oxygen can dissolve in seawater at this salinity than can dissolve in freshwater at the same temperature. In deltas, salinity varies considerably (from 0.5 to 35 ppt), depending on the amount of freshwater flowing in from rivers. Salinity decreases in spring due to rain and snowmelt, as these freshwater sources dilute the seawater. It increases in summer due to evaporation, which removes water vapor, leaving salt behind. For these reasons, oxygen concentrations vary in bays and estuaries (coastal river valleys flooded by oceans) due to shifts in temperature and salinity.

Around the world, many coral reefs—underwater environments that are home to colorful fish, sea turtles, sea snakes, sea grasses, and countless other life-forms—are turning into dead zones. In this photo, a lizard fish swims through a dead coral reef off the island of Bonaire in the Caribbean Sea.

Salt water is denser than freshwater, which leads to stratification. In gulfs, bays, and deltas, a layer of lighter freshwater sits on top of a heavier layer of salt water. Stratification prevents mixing and leads to lower oxygen concentrations on the bottom and in the sediments, where salinity is higher and water is denser. Because salinities (and therefore oxygen concentrations) are so variable in gulfs, bays, and deltas, many organisms in these ecosystems are adapted to survive in a relatively wide range of salinities and oxygen concentrations.

NATURAL DEAD ZONES

Some bodies of water naturally have extremely low levels of dissolved oxygen, or none at all, at the bottom, in and just above the sediments. These regions are naturally occurring dead zones. They form when water flow into a basin is restricted, preventing oxygen from entering and mixing with the water. The Black Sea, a large body of water between Europe and Asia, has a naturally occurring dead zone. The narrow Bosporus Strait, which connects the Black Sea to the Mediterranean Sea, is the Black Sea's only source of salty water. The strait has high sills, or underwater ridges, at both ends. These sills block the flow of salt water into the sea. The Baltic Sea does receive freshwater from several rivers. However, stratification and wave action keep the oxygen near the top of the water, and little or no oxygen reaches the bottom. Another natural dead zone is located in Saanich Inlet on Vancouver Island, off the southwestern coast of Canada. Near its mouth, Saanich Inlet has a 230-foot (70 m) sill, which restricts Pacific Ocean water from flowing in and mixing with water at the bottom of the inlet. Without mixing, this bottom water remains very low in oxygen.

Dead zones called oxygen minimum zones (OMZs) occur naturally in about 2 percent of the oceans, particularly in the eastern Pacific and northern Indian Oceans. OMZs are found approximately 1,600 feet (488 m) below the surface. OMZs develop as organic matter (such as waste matter and dead organisms) sinks from the sunlit surface into dark waters. Bacteria break down the organic matter, depleting the oxygen supply. Natural OMZs can last for thousands of years. Oceanographer Lisa Levin describes one OMZ that she and a fellow oceanographer viewed from a submersible (underwater vehicle) while studying the slope of Volcano 7. This underwater mountain lies 200 miles (322 km) west of Acapulco, Mexico. At the bottom of the mountain, she observed a variety of life-forms, including "dense groupings of crabs, shrimp, brittle stars and sponges." But in the OMZ, Levin observed that "as we moved up the mountain's slope, the rocks suddenly looked barren, covered with the merest fuzz of life." Oxygen readings in the barren zone were only 0.1 ppm.

EUTROPHICATION

The process by which a water body receives excess nutrients and becomes hypoxic is called eutrophication. The increase in nutrients can be either natural or cultural (human-made). In ponds and lakes, natural eutrophication occurs over time. As a pond or lake ages, it fills with sediment, which washes in as soil erodes from the surrounding land. The water gradually becomes shallower and more nutrient-rich. New ecosystems develop in the body of water in a predictable manner. At first, the pond or lake contains mostly water. As more nutrients enter the water, more plants grow there. At some point, the body becomes a wetland, such as a marsh filled with grasses or a swamp filled with trees. Eventually, the wetland fills completely with plants and soil and becomes dry land.

Cultural eutrophication results from nutrients added by farming and other human activity. Because it occurs much more rapidly than natural eutrophication, it causes environmental damage, including algal blooms, the contamination of drinking water, and hypoxia.

MAPPING AND MEASURING DEAD ZONES

The US National Aeronautics and Space Administration (NASA) can locate and map dead zones from space using satellites. On its dead zone maps, such as the one shown below, NASA scientists use colors to portray different concentrations of phytoplankton. This makes it easier for viewers to see where the plankton concentrations are at their highest and lowest. Maps show the densest phytoplankton concentrations in red, with decreasing densities shown in orange and then yellow. Every spring and summer, as phytoplankton growth explodes in the Gulf of Mexico, satellite photos show large areas of red and orange. These areas decline every fall and winter as growth slows or stops.

From the ocean surface, scientists map dead zones by measuring levels of dissolved oxygen. In the Gulf of Mexico, scientists also locate dead zones by conducting an annual ground-fish survey from the Texas–Mexico border, at the far west of the Gulf, east to the Florida Keys. They sample almost three hundred separate points along the way, dragging a fishing net across the bottom of the Gulf to determine what species and how many animals of each are present. In June 2013, the research vessel *Oregon II* brought up a nearly empty net (called a water haul) from a sampling location 60 miles (97 km) off the Louisiana coast and 150 miles (241 km) west of the Mississippi River delta. A water haul indicates a dead zone. Scientists on board the ship confirmed that the zone was dead by measuring levels of dissolved oxygen, temperature, and salinity.

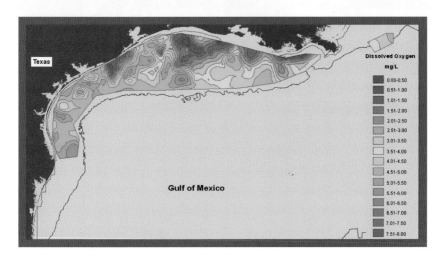

3 THE CORN CONNECTION

The size of the Gulf of Mexico dead zone is mainly determined by the amount of fertilizer flowing in from the Mississippi River. It is also related to the amount of rainfall each year along the Mississippi watershed (the land area drained by the river). In years with heavy rains and flooding along the Mississippi (for example, 2008), more nutrients wash into the Gulf, resulting in a larger dead zone. In drought years, when rainfall is low, such as in 2009 and 2012, the dead zone area is much smaller.

Wind speed and direction also affect the size of the dead zone. As wind speed increases, more oxygen will mix into the dead zone and decrease its size. Wind direction will help determine the extent of the zone and whether it moves along the coast or spreads farther out to sea. Finally, water stratification helps form and maintain the dead zone. Less dense freshwater from the Mississippi River does not mix with deeper, denser salt water. Instead, it forms a lid over the

In the Gulf of Mexico, fishers and shrimpers have to take their boats farther and farther out to sea to find animals during the summer dead zone season. Many fishing boat operators have gone broke.

salt water, preventing oxygen from moving into the depths.

Evidence shows the Gulf of Mexico dead zone is growing. The few times a dead zone occurred in the Gulf in the 1950s, each one measured about 1,158 to 1,544 square miles (3,000 to 4,000 sq. km). By the twenty-first century, the dead zone was many times larger, averaging 5,176 square miles (13,406 sq. km) in the five years between 2008 and 2013. The largest dead zone ever measured in the Gulf was 8,494 square miles (22,000 sq. km) in 2002. The growth is due to increased levels of nitrogen in the Gulf, which have tripled since the 1960s.

Dean Blanchard is president and owner of Dean Blanchard Seafood in Grand Isle, Louisiana. Members of Blanchard's family have worked as fishers in the Gulf of Mexico for five generations. Since 2007 he has seen major changes in the Gulf's annual dead zone. It is hurting the summer fishing season, forcing many people to find other kinds of work. Around Grand Isle, hypoxia in the dead zone particularly affects shrimp, crabs, and red drum (a fish preferred by recreational fishers). Sea bobs (a small species of shrimp) are completely gone. The animals move away from shore when oxygen declines. "Usually, you could throw a baseball at [the boats] from the beach. They're just right there. When the dead zone comes, they're a hundred miles [161 km] out," Blanchard says.

THE MARB AND THE MRB

The gigantic watershed that empties into the Gulf of Mexico is the largest in the United States and the third largest in the world. Only the Amazon River watershed in South America and the Congo River watershed in Africa are larger. The Gulf watershed consists of two drainage systems: the Mississippi River and the smaller Atchafalaya River, which branches off the Mississippi and enters the Gulf to the west of the Mississippi. This combined drainage is called the Mississippi-Atchafalaya River Basin, or MARB. The Mississippi River Basin on its own is called the MRB.

The Mississippi River begins as a tiny stream leaving Lake Itasca in northern Minnesota. It takes a wandering course, snaking southward for about 2,350 miles (3,782 km) before finally entering the Gulf of Mexico south of New Orleans, Louisiana. Along the way, it drains parts of thirty-one states and two Canadian provinces. Its tributaries (waterways that flow into the river) include several other large rivers, including the Missouri, Ohio, and Arkansas. It forms partial borders for ten states and drains 41 percent of the United States and 15 percent of North America.

The Atchafalaya River is a distributary of the Mississippi rather than a tributary. That is, instead of feeding into the Mississippi, it branches off and enters the Gulf separately. The Atchafalaya is 135 miles (217 km) long. Its watershed comprises 1.4 million acres (567,000 hectares) of hardwood forest. Half of North America's migratory waterfowl live here part of the year. The watershed is home to more than three hundred species of birds and hosts birds that make yearly migrations to and from the tropics.

People establish cities and industries along rivers for access to freshwater and transportation. Over the years, engineering changes

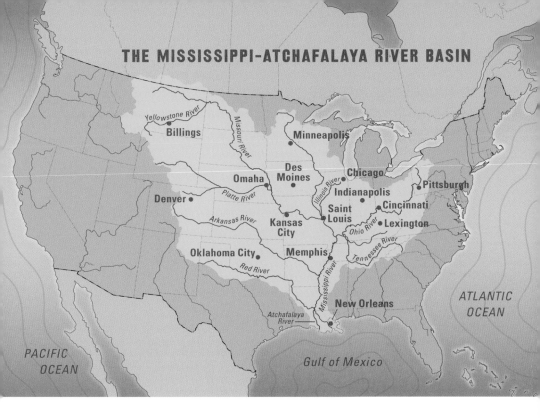

THE MISSISSIPPI-ATCHAFALAYA RIVER BASIN

have highly modified the Mississippi. Engineers have straightened the course of the river to make it easier for large barges and other ships to navigate. Communities have also built dams (barriers across the river) and levees (walls) to control seasonal river flooding. They have built chambers called locks to allow barges and other river traffic to travel past dams. This construction has destroyed wetlands such as swamps and marshes. It has also killed off many plant and animal species for which these wetlands were prime nesting and feeding grounds. The loss of wetlands and the straightening of the river have increased the rate of river flow, sending more water and sediment more rapidly into the Mississippi Delta.

For the most part, the Atchafalaya has remained a wild, natural river surrounded by forests, wetlands, and a rich bird and wildlife habitat. But in the mid-twentieth century, the US Army Corps of Engineers built floodwater control structures in its central basin. The structures open during floods to allow Mississippi River water to flow into the Atchafalaya Basin to prevent downstream flooding on the Mississippi. Intensive logging of the region's cypress-tupelo swamps has increased the amount of silt entering the Atchafalaya. (These swamps provide, among other things, the cypress mulch that many Americans use in their gardens.) Also, beginning in the mid-twentieth century, the oil industry drilled oil and gas wells, dredged canals for oil crew boats, and built drilling rigs and pipelines near the Atchafalaya. The industry is still active, and oil spills and leaks still plague the area. Oil drilling and transport also contribute pollutants such as silt and mercury to the river. Although the Atchafalaya River is very small compared to the Mississippi, its pollutants contribute to the formation of the Gulf dead zone.

ONTO THE FIELDS AND DOWN THE RIVER

The growing Gulf dead zone directly correlates with increasing use of nitrogen fertilizers along the Mississippi River. Agriculture—mostly from corn production in midwestern states—accounts for 70 percent of the Gulf's nitrogen pollution.

Nine states in the Mississippi watershed (Iowa, Illinois, Indiana, Missouri, Arkansas, Kentucky, Tennessee, Ohio, and Mississippi) are major agricultural states. Every spring and fall, farmers there apply large amounts of fertilizer to their fields. Approximately half of this fertilizer runs off the fields into streams and rivers. It ultimately reaches the Gulf of Mexico, where it contributes to formation of the annual dead zone.

According to the US Geological Survey (USGS), a government agency that gathers and analyzes scientific data about Earth and the environment, Iowa and Illinois together contribute 35 percent of the nitrogen entering the Gulf. Iowa alone, which produces approximately $12 billion worth of corn, soybeans, and other crops annually, may contribute as much as 25 percent. And the amount of nitrogen entering the river is increasing. A USGS study at Clinton, Iowa, showed a 76 percent increase in nitrogen entering the river between 1980 and 2008. For the entire Mississippi River watershed, this nitrogen loading has increased by 150 times since 1900.

HOW THE GULF OF MEXICO DEAD ZONE FORMS

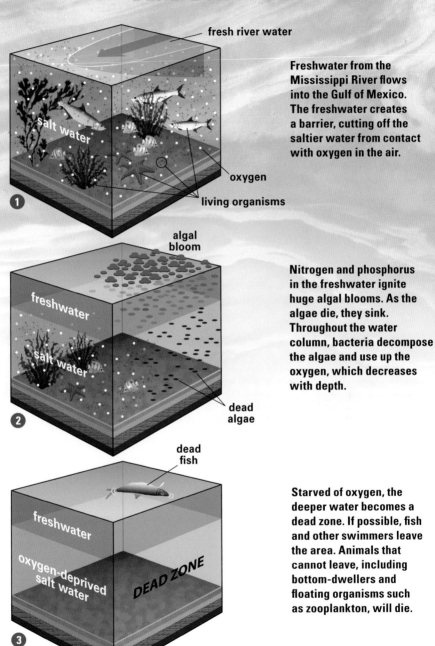

fresh river water

salt water

oxygen

living organisms

1

Freshwater from the Mississippi River flows into the Gulf of Mexico. The freshwater creates a barrier, cutting off the saltier water from contact with oxygen in the air.

algal bloom

freshwater

salt water

dead algae

2

Nitrogen and phosphorus in the freshwater ignite huge algal blooms. As the algae die, they sink. Throughout the water column, bacteria decompose the algae and use up the oxygen, which decreases with depth.

dead fish

freshwater

oxygen-deprived salt water

DEAD ZONE

3

Starved of oxygen, the deeper water becomes a dead zone. If possible, fish and other swimmers leave the area. Animals that cannot leave, including bottom-dwellers and floating organisms such as zooplankton, will die.

The Corn Belt is a region of heavy corn production covering most of Iowa and parts of Illinois, Indiana, Michigan, Minnesota, Missouri, Nebraska, Ohio, South Dakota, and Wisconsin. Compared to most other crops, corn requires large amounts of nitrogen to grow. Many Corn Belt farmers prefer to apply the nutrient in the fall, when fertilizer prices are lower than they are in spring. Some farmers apply more nitrogen than is needed in the fall to make up for possible losses due to runoff. Much of that runoff occurs in early spring before new corn begins to grow and when snow melts and heavy spring rains wash fertilizers and sediment into streams.

Flooding further compounds the runoff problem. In major flood years, such as 2008 and 2010, record amounts of nitrogen from midwestern fields flow down the Mississippi and into the Gulf. Only Hurricane Dolly, which reached the Gulf Coast at approximately the same time as the 2008 floodwaters, prevented a record-breaking dead zone that year. Dolly's winds helped mix the water, adding oxygen and diminishing the dead zone. (On the other hand, hurricanes also stir up pollution and sediment, which can make dead zones worse.)

In many midwestern states, a drainage process called tiling further contributes to runoff. To drain a field, farmers use perforated pipes called tile. They bury the tile 3 to 4 feet (0.9 to 1.2 m) below the soil surface. Water enters the pipes through the perforations. The pipes empty straight into waterways and eventually into the Mississippi. All of this water contains dissolved nitrogen. Before tiling began in the Midwest, water passed through natural filters, such as grasses and plant roots, which trapped nutrients, keeping them in local ecosystems. In the twenty-first century, 90 percent of nutrients entering the water through tiling systems enter waterways that eventually run to the Gulf.

In the late nineteenth century, Iowa farmers began draining their state's wetlands to make more farmland. As of 2015, more than 90 percent of Iowa's wetlands—the most of any state along the Mississippi—have been converted to agriculture. Iowa's tiling system contributes significantly to nitrogen runoff. However, other midwestern states—particularly Illinois, Indiana, Ohio, Minnesota, and Michigan—are also heavily tiled. According to Resources for the Future—an organization that does research on the environment, energy, and natural resources—tile drainage in the Corn Belt has been increasing rapidly since the 1990s.

NUTRIENT POLLUTION

The US Department of Agriculture (USDA) calculates that 23 percent of US farmland is planted in corn, and corn production is responsible for 40 percent of the fertilizer use in the United States. In the MRB, corn farming is the primary source of nitrogen pollution and the second-largest source of phosphorus pollution. (Animal manure is the largest source.) Corn farming is also the major contributor to algal blooms and the resulting hypoxia in the Gulf of Mexico. Fertilization of corn and soybean fields accounts for half of the nitrogen and one-fourth of the phosphorus entering the Gulf. Corn and soybeans are usually planted in rotation. That is, farmers usually plant a field with corn one year and soybeans the next. But because corn is much more heavily fertilized, it accounts for most of the nutrient pollution—97 percent of the nitrogen and 80 percent of the phosphorus—from those fields.

Annual nitrogen fertilizer use in the United States increased by 455 percent between 1960 and 2005. Much of this fertilizer was used on corn. This trend has occurred for several reasons. First, modern high-yield corn varieties require larger amounts of fertilizer than earlier varieties. In addition, ever since farming began in the Midwest, farmers have steadily plowed up prairie grasses. Without grass roots to hold rich topsoil in place, it is easily eroded, or carried away by rain and wind. The remaining soil is less nutrient-rich, requiring the application of

ANNUAL NITROGEN FERTILIZER USE IN THE UNITED STATES INCREASED BY 455 PERCENT BETWEEN 1960 AND 2005. MUCH OF THIS FERTILIZER WAS USED ON CORN.

more fertilizer. In addition, growing populations in the United States and around the world require increasing amounts of food. This means that farmers must produce more crops on existing fields—so they apply more fertilizer.

For a time in the 1990s, midwestern farmers began to use less fertilizer, in part because they found that applying more fertilizer no longer led to significant increases in crop yields. They were also concerned about rising fertilizer costs and pollution of the soil and water. Farmers began to plant more corn—and use more fertilizer—again in the early 2000s. But most of this corn does not feed people. Forty percent of US corn goes into production of ethanol, a type of alcohol that is used to power vehicles. Another 36 percent feeds cattle, hogs, and chickens.

By the time people eat the meat and dairy products resulting from corn-fed animals, most of the corn's calories have been lost. Typically, about 90 percent of the energy contained in one level of a food chain either remains in that level or is lost to the environment as heat. Only 10 percent travels to the next level. So the longer the food chain, the less energy is available at the top. If you eat a hamburger, you are in the food chain "corn to cow to human." So if the corn level has one hundred units of food energy, the cow level gets ten, and the human level gets only one. If you eat an ear

SHRIMP VERSUS CORN

The Gulf of Mexico produces most of the shrimp (82 percent in 2010) in the United States. But fertilizer runoff decreases shrimp production. Meanwhile, corn production is increasing, hurting shrimp production even more. As former shrimper Dirk Guidry explains, "Corn is a more important crop in the U.S. than shrimp. You have to have corn, but you don't have to have shrimp."

of corn, the food chain has only two levels (corn to human). One hundred units of food energy from the corn would provide ten to the human—ten times the energy of a three-level chain. Thus eating the corn (or any vegetable) directly is much more efficient and results in more food for more people than does eating meat.

In addition, US meat production produces manure. Cattle, hogs, chickens, and turkeys are raised at factory farms called concentrated animal feeding operations (CAFOs). These operations produce approximately 500 million tons (454 million metric tons) of manure per year. This is more than three times the amount of sewage produced by the human population of the United States. The waste is not treated. Farmers typically store it either in manure pits or lagoons until it has matured, or partially broken down. Then farmers apply much of it to farm fields as fertilizer. Farmers often apply more fertilizer than needed. The excess runs off into the waterways that

Hogs are crowded into pens at a concentrated animal feeding operation in Iowa. Farmers feed the animals corn, which is grown using massive amounts of fertilizer—the key cause of the dead zone problem in the Gulf of Mexico. In addition, the animals produce vast amounts of manure, which itself is used as fertilizer. If allowed to wash into waterways, manure can contribute to the growth of dead zones as well.

feed into the Mississippi and ultimately the Gulf of Mexico. In this way, animal manure becomes a part of the nutrient pollution that fuels dead zones.

THE ETHANOL MANDATE

The gasoline we use to fuel our cars, trucks, buses, and other vehicles is made from petroleum, and it releases large amounts of carbon dioxide into the air. This extra carbon traps heat in the atmosphere and has led to climate change on Earth. To try to reduce the amount of carbon entering the air from US cars and other vehicles, the US Congress created the Renewable Fuel Standard (RFS) program in 2005. This program mandated that manufacturers add 7.5 billion gallons (28 billion liters) of

MORE MEATLESS DAYS

Environmentalists say that if more people switched to a vegetarian diet, Earth and its inhabitants would be in far better shape. People who eat lots of vegetables, fruits, and whole grains are less likely to develop heart disease, cancer, diabetes, and other health problems than people with meat-heavy diets. We could also cut down on the use of freshwater—a precious and endangered resource—by eating less meat and eating more vegetables. Consider that it takes approximately 1,850 gallons (7,003 liters) of water to produce a single pound (453 grams) of beef and only about 39 gallons (148 liters) of water to produce a pound of vegetables. According to the Meatless Monday organization, which encourages people to give up meat one day per week, we could cut water consumption in the United States by 58 percent per person if everyone switched to a vegetarian diet. Raising meat also produces more greenhouse gases than growing vegetables and grains, and it requires more energy from fossil fuels. Finally, if we cut down on meat, farmers could grow less corn and therefore use less nitrogen on their crops.

A Michigan woman fills her gas tank with fuel containing 85 percent ethanol. Ethanol, which is made from corn, is better for the planet than ordinary gasoline, because it releases less carbon dioxide when burned. The US government encourages the use of ethanol. But growing more corn to produce more ethanol contributes to the creation of dead zones.

renewable fuel—specifically ethanol, made from corn and other plants—to US gasoline by 2012. In addition to cutting down on carbon emissions, the program was designed to make the United States less dependent on foreign sources of petroleum. And corn is an easy-to-grow, renewable resource. Petroleum, on the other hand, is nonrenewable.

Congress expanded the ethanol mandate with the Energy Independence and Security Act (EISA) of 2007. The EISA program, overseen by the EPA, upped the amount of corn ethanol to be added to gasoline every year from 9 billion gallons (34 billion liters) in 2008 to 36 billion gallons (136 billion liters) by 2022. To meet the demand for ethanol, US farmers converted more than 23 million acres (9.3 million hectares) of wetlands and grasslands to corn production between 2008 and 2011. But increases in corn production have led to increased runoff into the Mississippi and increased hypoxia in the Gulf of Mexico.

FUEL FROM NITROGEN WASTE

Researchers from Stanford University in California are working on a method to remove excess nitrogen from polluted water and then use bacteria to transform the nitrogen into nitrous oxide gas, which can be used for fuel. The initial project, called Coupled Aerobic-anoxic Nitrous Decomposition Operation (CANDO), is a cooperative venture between Stanford and the Delta Diablo Sanitation District in Antioch, California. If successful, the process represents a win-win for the environment. It will decrease air pollution by using up excess nitrous oxide, a gas that would otherwise become a pollutant and contribute to climate change. It will also help farmers around the world remove waste nitrogen from their local waterways, thereby decreasing the number of dead zones.

According to geographer Simon Donner and atmospheric scientist Christopher Kucharik, the continuing demand for corn ethanol will likely cause up to 34 percent more nitrogen pollution along the MRB by 2022. Donner and Kucharik say that the only way to increase ethanol production while decreasing nitrogen runoff is for Americans to stop eating meat. This would free up corn for ethanol rather than for cattle feed.

Most US corn not used in fuel or animal feed is exported. In the 2013–2014 marketing year, the United States was the world's leading corn exporter. It sold corn to more than one hundred countries, with most going to Japan, Mexico, and Korea. Only a tiny fraction of corn becomes food for US citizens—and most of that goes into high-fructose corn syrup. Food manufacturers use this corn product as an

> THE CORN *CROP* IS HIGHLY PRODUCTIVE, BUT THE CORN *SYSTEM* IS ALIGNED TO FEED CARS AND ANIMALS INSTEAD OF FEEDING PEOPLE.
>
> JONATHAN FOLEY

ingredient in processed foods such as breakfast cereals, cookies, and soft drinks, adding very little nutritional value to these foods. If all the corn from an average Iowa cornfield was grown for people to eat, the field could sustain fourteen people per acre (0.4 hectares). However, with the current diversion of corn into fuel and animal feed, the field sustains only three people per acre. According to Jonathan Foley, writing for *Scientific American*, "The corn *crop* is highly productive, but the corn *system* is aligned to feed cars and animals instead of feeding people."

4 A PLANETARY PROBLEM

ccording to Robert Diaz of the College of William and Mary, "The primary culprit in marine environments is nitrogen and, nowadays, the biggest contributor of nitrogen to marine systems is agriculture. It's the same scenario all over the world."

The recurring dead zone in the Gulf of Mexico is the largest in the United States and one of the largest in the world. But dead zones are coming to more places, spreading farther, and staying longer. According to a study in the journal *Science*, "Creeping dead zones" have doubled every decade since the 1960s, mostly due to agricultural pollution. In 1960 the world had forty-nine known dead zones. That number had increased to 405 in 2007 and to more than 550 by late 2014. Most dead zones are located along the East Coast and Gulf Coast of the United States, along the coastlines of Japan and the Koreas in Asia, and along the coasts of nations bordering the Baltic Sea in Europe. A 2008 study showed that oxygen levels in parts of the world's open oceans have also been declining since the 1950s.

THE CHESAPEAKE DEAD ZONE

After the Gulf of Mexico's dead zone, the second-largest dead zone in the United States is in Chesapeake Bay. This bay receives 300 million pounds (136 million kilograms) of nitrogen pollution per year and is on a "dirty waters" list created by the EPA. The Chesapeake Bay dead zone results from a combination of urbanization and agriculture. Nitrogen and phosphorus come into the bay from poultry farms, urban and industrial wastewater, and air pollution (mostly nitrous oxides that dissolve into the water).

Problems in the bay became visible in the 1980s. That's when researchers noted a loss of bay grasses; reduced numbers of striped bass, shad, oysters, and blue crabs in the bay; cloudy water; and summer dead zones that were becoming larger and lasting longer. In the following decades, the dead zone began to affect Atlantic croaker, white perch, striped bass, and summer flounder—all important

EARTH'S MAJOR DEAD ZONES

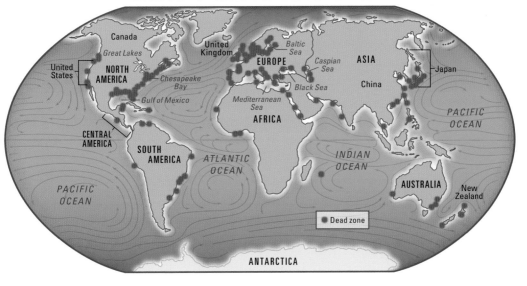

commercial fishes. The dead zone continues to appear each year. Oxygen levels are lowest during midsummer in the deep waters in the middle of the bay. Stress causes the fish there to begin moving away when oxygen drops to 4 ppm. Low oxygen levels also stress and kill bottom-dwelling organisms, such as worms, clams, and crabs, on which the fish feed.

The dead zone in the Chesapeake Bay could grow larger because of the Conowingo Dam on the Susquehanna River in northeastern Maryland, which has not been properly dredged or maintained. The reservoir behind the dam contains approximately 175 million tons (159 million metric tons) of polluted sediment, including clay, silt, fertilizer runoff, sewage runoff, and toxic chemicals that have built up since the dam opened in 1929. During large storms, which occur every four or five years, some of the sediment washes over the dam, polluting the river downstream and the Chesapeake Bay into which it empties. Members of a group called the Clean Chesapeake Coalition fear the next big storm could send all or most of this trapped sediment over the dam and into the bay, causing a catastrophe. Others disagree. They say that nitrogen entering the river from farm runoff, sewage, and other sources—not sediment from the dam—is the major source of pollution reaching the bay.

COASTAL HABS

On their own, algal blooms can cause hypoxia and suffocate fish, but some blooms are also toxic to plants, animals, and people. Harmful algal blooms (HABs) are a large and growing problem, causing damage to corals, sea grasses, and bottom-dwelling animals around the world. Experts say that HABs cause at least $82 million of damage per year in the United States alone, mostly in increased public health costs and decreased profits for commercial fisheries. Other damage includes illness and death of marine animals due to clogged gills, smothering, and toxic effects. Societal damage includes the loss of recreational opportunities (swimming, fishing, and boating) and fewer tourists at beaches. In some parts of the world, people who live on seacoasts rely on subsistence fishing. That is, they catch only enough fish for their own use. During HABs, this part of their livelihood is lost. HABs also result in lowered property values.

HABs occur along all US coasts, but six states have been especially impacted. In Washington, in 2002 and 2003, HABs caused a season-long closing of the state's razor clam and Dungeness crab fisheries and resulted in losses of $10 to $12 million. In Hawaii yearly HABs have resulted in high cleanup costs, lost hotel business, and lowered real estate values. Annual losses are approximately $16 million. HABs in Maine and Massachusetts in 2005 produced a toxin that paralyzes humans and other animals. This led to the closure of shellfish fisheries in both states, with losses of at least $18 million in

Karenia brevis, a harmful algal bloom, creates red tide along a beach in Queensland, Australia. Red tides can kill many kinds of animals.

Massachusetts and $4.9 million in Maine.

Along the Texas and Florida coasts, the major HAB culprit is an alga called *Karenia brevis*, which causes red tide (so named because it turns the water a reddish color). Off Florida's west coast, red tides recur almost every year, killing fish, birds, and marine mammals and causing respiratory problems in humans. The estimated cost from Florida's red tide is $19 to $32 million per year. A 2000 *Karenia* bloom off the Texas coast caused $9.9 million in lost revenue.

THE ESTIMATED COST FROM FLORIDA'S RED TIDE IS $19 TO $32 MILLION PER YEAR.

HABs are not just an American problem. They occur in China, Japan, Brazil, Australia, and many other countries. According to a paper in the *Polish Journal of Environmental Studies*, HABs have become "one of the most serious health risks of the 21st century."

NOT-SO-GREAT LAKES

In summer 2014, the five hundred thousand citizens of Toledo, Ohio, on the southwestern edge of Lake Erie, were unable to drink city-supplied water for several days. Toledo's drinking water comes from Lake Erie, one of the five Great Lakes. Toxic blooms of the bacterium *Microcystis* had contaminated the lake that summer. Toledo city officials instituted a do-not-drink advisory, while sending water samples to laboratories for testing. The Ohio governor declared a state of emergency. Residents rushed to stock up on bottled water, and some communities set up centers to distribute safe donated drinking water. The increase in *Microcystis* was partly due to the presence, since the 1980s, of quagga and zebra mussels in the lake. They are both invasive species, which means they are not native to the United States. (They reached the country by attaching themselves to ships that traveled into the Great Lakes from affected waters elsewhere.) These shellfish won't eat *Microcystis*, so it had built up in the lake. Warmer temperatures due to climate change

Microcystis blooms in Lake Erie in the summer of 2014 contaminated drinking water supplies. Citizens of Toledo, Ohio, could not drink city-supplied water for several days.

also stimulated the toxic blooms, according to Gary Fahnenstiel, an ecologist at Michigan Technological University. But the main cause of the algal blooms was runoff from surrounding agricultural and urban areas.

Lake Erie is shallow, so it warms and cools earlier in the year than the other four Great Lakes. Because the surface warms earlier in spring, summer water stratification also occurs earlier, setting the stage for algal blooms. Erie also receives the most phosphorus of all the Great Lakes. In the 1960s and 1970s, Lake Erie was declared dead or dying, due to summer dead zones that caused massive fish kills. Its western and central basins were filled with blue-green bacteria and coarse fish—organisms that can withstand very low oxygen levels. The lake recovered, thanks to a multibillion-dollar cleanup by the United States and Canada.

The 2014 Lake Erie *Microcystis* bloom, although damaging, was only half as large as the record-breaking Lake Erie bloom of 2011. The bloom reached beneath the surface into the lake's cold central basin.

That dead zone measured 2,000 square miles (5,180 sq. km), more than three times larger than any previous bloom. Scientists say the bloom was most likely a sign of things to come.

A study of the 2011 bloom showed that two long-term trends in agricultural practice in areas surrounding the lake had increased runoff in the Lake Erie watershed in the preceding years. The first practice was fall fertilizer application. When fertilizer is applied in the fall rather than in the spring, much more of it runs off and often it must be reapplied. The second practice was broadcasting fertilizer onto the soil surface (as either dry fertilizer or liquid spray) rather than injecting it into the ground, which also cuts down on runoff. These trends correlate with the 218 percent increase in phosphorus loading in the lake between 1995 and 2011. Also, the study showed that warm temperatures and low winds over the lake before and during the 2011 bloom had decreased circulation and mixing and led to conditions favoring blooms. Higher temperatures are also likely to increase in the future as climate change progresses.

Another Great Lake, Lake Michigan, also has dead zones. The major problem in Lake Michigan occurs in Green Bay, an arm of the lake that reaches into northeastern Wisconsin. The bay receives one-third of the lake's nutrient load, mostly phosphorus from farms and construction sites. Farm phosphorus comes from soil and phosphorus-containing fertilizers. About 19 percent of the phosphorus washing into lakes comes from construction sites. All soil, especially organic matter such as dead leaves, contains phosphorus. When soil is disturbed during construction, the sediment particles that erode into streams and lakes have phosphorus attached to them.

AROUND THE WORLD

Signs of eutrophication are increasing around the world. Scientists have identified hundreds of problem areas that may soon become full-fledged dead zones. These include spots along the west coasts of

Central and South America and along the coastlines of Australia and Great Britain. The coasts of China, Japan, and many parts of Europe already have dead zones. Many of these areas are in industrialized countries, and most have arisen since the 1950s. Like those in the Gulf of Mexico and Chesapeake Bay, most of these dead zones are annual. They appear in summer, when the water is warm and stratified, and break up in the autumn, when water cools and winds mix oxygen back into the water. But some dead zones, particularly in more tropical regions, last all year long.

The worst dead zones are in the Baltic Sea, which is surrounded by nine European countries (Finland, Sweden, Russia, Estonia, Latvia, Lithuania, Poland, Germany, and Denmark). All of these countries contribute nutrients to the sea, mostly through runoff of nitrogen and phosphorus fertilizers. Sewage and sediment also enter the sea from urban areas. Fisheries in the sea have been wiped out and have not recovered. The Kattegat, an arm of the North Sea bounded by Denmark and Sweden, also has a large dead zone. Its lobster industry has collapsed, and bottom-dwelling fish populations have been reduced.

Lakes and rivers around the world are also affected. In 2004 a toxic algal bloom in Lake Victoria left five hundred thousand people in Kisumu, Kenya, temporarily without drinking water. In 2007 an algal bloom on China's Lake Taihu left more than two million people in the city of Wuxi without piped drinking water for more than a week. When the Murray River in southeastern Australia suffered a 497-mile-long (800 km) toxic bloom in 2009, officials issued a red alert, warning people not to drink the water.

IN 2004 A TOXIC ALGAL BLOOM IN LAKE VICTORIA LEFT FIVE HUNDRED THOUSAND PEOPLE IN KISUMU, KENYA, TEMPORARILY WITHOUT DRINKING WATER.

Australian scientists say that dead zones in Australia are not yet as serious as in some other parts of the world, but scientists are still worried. Oxygen levels off the southeastern coast of Australia

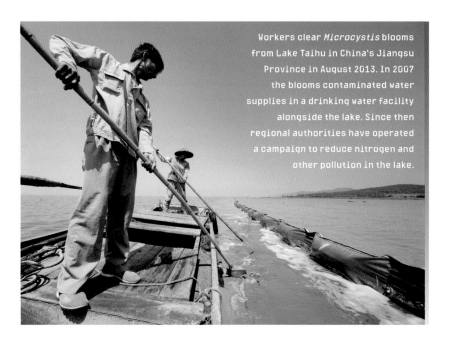

Workers clear *Microcystis* blooms from Lake Taihu in China's Jiangsu Province in August 2013. In 2007 the blooms contaminated water supplies in a drinking water facility alongside the lake. Since then regional authorities have operated a campaign to reduce nitrogen and other pollution in the lake.

are low. Oxygen depletion from nutrient runoff is killing fish and other organisms on the Great Barrier Reef, the world's most impressive coral reef, attracting millions of tourists each year. Ove Hoegh-Guldberg, a professor of marine science at the University of Queensland in northeastern Australia, points out that nutrients entering the ocean along the coasts eventually settle into deeper areas, where they also worsen deep-ocean dead zones. According to Hoegh-Guldberg, "Ocean ecosystems are in a lot of trouble and it bears all the hallmarks of human interference. . . . We are changing the way the Earth's oceans work, shifting them to entirely new states, which we have not seen before."

OIL AND WATER

Around the world, oil spills contribute to dead zones. Spills are common in coastal environments, although usually only the largest spills receive widespread news coverage. Major Gulf of Mexico spills include the 2010 *Deepwater Horizon* disaster, during which 206 million gallons (780 million liters) of oil gushed into the Gulf for three months after an explosion at an offshore oil rig, about 42 miles (68 km) off the coast of Louisiana. The 1979 *Ixtoc I* spill released 140 million gallons (530 million liters) of oil into the Gulf over a nine-month period. In 1989 the oil tanker *Exxon Valdez* spilled 11 million gallons (42 million liters) of crude oil into Alaska's Prince William Sound. The spill ultimately fouled more than 1,000 miles (1,609 km) of beaches and killed hundreds of thousands of seabirds, seals, and other animals. However, these huge spills make up a relatively small proportion of the total oil spilled around the world annually. Most oil spills are smaller, but they occur more frequently. They originate at pipelines, trains transporting oil, oil-processing facilities, oil wells, and other oil-industry vessels and structures. According to Amnesty International (AI), a human rights organization, over the last fifty years, an estimated 1.5 million tons (1.36 million metric tons) of oil have spilled into the Niger delta, the area in Nigeria where the Niger River meets the Atlantic Ocean. This equals about one *Exxon Valdez–*level spill per year, explains AI.

Oil has specific toxic effects on plants, animals, and humans, and it causes hypoxia as well. When oil spills at sea, it coats the ocean surface, preventing oxygen from entering the water and suffocating organisms trapped beneath it. Spills can be especially damaging to sea life near shore, in the wetlands and deltas that serve as nurseries for young ocean organisms. After the *Deepwater Horizon* spill, marine scientist Monty Graham and a team from the Dauphin Island (Alabama) Sea Lab trawled the near-shore waters of the Gulf. "In the low oxygen, all we got were sea stars. The fishes were up against the shore," Graham said. "In the same time frame, people started to see large sharks cruising in unprecedented numbers up against the shore. The low oxygen [had] pushed the prey up against the shore and the sharks [were] cruising to take advantage of that."

During oil spills, oil keeps sunlight from penetrating into the ocean and decreases photosynthesis in algae deeper in the water. The oil eventually breaks down or sinks and coats shallow-water

COMPLEXITY PREVENTS
EASY PREDICTION

The complex interactions between oil and water make it difficult for scientists to determine exactly how an oil spill will affect the size and severity of dead zones. For instance, in some cases, oil spills may actually shrink dead zones by limiting the amount of light entering the water and thus limiting algal growth. Oil is also toxic to some types of algae and becomes more toxic when it interacts with sunlight. For this reason, an oil spill could end up killing off algae and decreasing the likelihood of dead zone formation. At the same time, other characteristics of an oil spill can make dead zones more likely. Each oil spill must be considered separately.

---

sediments. Meanwhile, surface algal blooms occur because the oil has killed the zooplankton that feed on the algae. During the *Deepwater Horizon* spill, oil was released in plumes deep underwater. Dead zones formed along the plumes as bacteria broke down the oil and used up the small amount of oxygen there.

Also during the *Deepwater Horizon* spill, up to one hundred thousand times the normal ocean levels of methane (an ingredient in natural gas) spewed out of the exploded well along with the oil. The methane settled in a layer between 3,280 and 4,265 feet (1,000 and 1,300 m) deep. Within a 5-mile (8 km) radius around the broken wellhead, oxygen levels declined by 30 percent as bacteria used the oxygen during respiration to break down the methane. Fish quickly moved out of the area toward the shore. The oil also spread outward, reaching the shores of five states. Around Dauphin Island, Alabama, researchers found depleted oxygen levels up to 40 miles (64 km) offshore.

In a report released four months after the spill, NOAA and EPA scientists reported that within 60 miles (97 km) of the broken well (which by then had been sealed), dissolved oxygen levels averaged 20

Oil from the *Deepwater Horizon* spill not only killed hundreds of thousands of animals but also worsened the Gulf dead zone. The oil coated the ocean surface, preventing oxygen and sunlight from reaching the water below. The oil also killed off animals that normally feed on algal blooms.

percent below average. The lowest level recorded was 3.5 ppm, a little higher than that of a true dead zone.

While photosynthesis and wind and wave action quickly replace surface oxygen after an oil spill, oxygen depletion may continue for years in the deeper ocean. "If you drive the oxygen down at 1,200 meters [3,937 feet], there is nothing to replace that oxygen rapidly," Graham says. "You might see . . . low oxygen . . . for years, maybe even decades."

GLOBAL WARMING

Climate change, caused largely by humans burning fossil fuels, threatens to increase dead zones. Warm water holds less oxygen than cool water, and ocean temperatures have been rising for several decades due to climate change. Scientists predict that OMZs will expand as oceans continue to warm. A recent study from the University of Copenhagen in Denmark indicates that as Earth warms, the biggest declines in oxygen in the oceans will occur in the Pacific Ocean off the coasts of Peru, Chile, and California and in the seas on both coasts of India.

DEFORMITIES IN THE DEAD ZONE

The 2010 *Deepwater Horizon* spill has caused long-term health damage to fish. Three years after the spill, many catches were still lower than before the spill. According to seafood processor Keath Ladner, of Hancock County, Mississippi, "I've seen the brown shrimp catch drop by two-thirds, and so far the white shrimp have been wiped out. . . . We are finding shrimp with tumors on their heads, and are seeing this every day."

Eighty miles (129 km) north of the spill, in Yscloskey and Pointe à la Hache, Louisiana, many oyster reefs are dead, and crabs and fish are harder to find. Although testing shows only trace amounts of petroleum in seafood from the Gulf, many people are afraid to eat it. The combination of lower demand for seafood and lower catches means that Gulf fishing communities are still being hard hit by the oil spill.

Gulf fishers such as Ladner are finding serious deformities in their catches, including eyeless crabs and shrimp, clawless crabs, and fish with lesions and oozing sores. Jim Cowan of Louisiana State University believes that these deformities are due to the animals' exposure to chemicals in petroleum. "The fishermen have never seen anything like this," Cowan said. "And in my 20 years working on red snapper, looking at somewhere between 20 and 30,000 fish, I've never seen anything like this either."

According to fishers Tracy Kuhns and Mike Roberts from Barataria, Louisiana, at least 50 percent of the shrimp caught in Barataria Bay in 2011 were eyeless. "At the height of the last white shrimp season, in September, one of our friends caught 400 pounds (181 kg) of these [eyeless shrimp]," Kuhns said.

These deformities suggest that oil has damaged the organisms' immune systems, the body processes by which animals fight off illnesses. This damage makes the creatures more vulnerable to other environmental stresses, including hypoxia.

Studies by Ralph Keeling and Hernan Garcia of the Scripps Institution of Oceanography in San Diego, California, verify that ocean oxygen levels are already falling and that they will fall more rapidly as global warming increases. The effects of hypoxia are beginning at the ocean surface and will eventually extend into deeper waters. Because water warms much more slowly than air or land, scientists say it will take several thousand years for oceans to feel the full effects of hypoxia. But some changes are already evident. For instance, global warming increases rainfall, which in turn increases runoff of nutrients from the land, leading to increased hypoxia. At the same time, warming increases the intensity of storms such as hurricanes, which can have the opposite effect, mixing the water and increasing oxygen levels—at least in the short term.

Carbon dioxide and other greenhouse gases are warming the planet. The oceans are getting warmer, which leads to lower oxygen levels there, since warm water holds less oxygen than cold water.

As ocean hypoxia due to climate change progresses, oceans will become unable to support many marine species. Many fish and shellfish species will die out, giving way to blooms of plankton. These food web changes will threaten or destroy ocean fisheries, many of which are already declining due to overfishing. Scientists warn that the widespread oxygen depletion caused by global warming will not be easily reversed. According to researcher Gary Shaffer of the University of Copenhagen, the only way to stop ocean dead zones from developing is to reduce fossil fuel emissions over the next several generations. But even if we do this, he cautions, some ocean warming and oxygen depletion are inevitable due to carbon emissions that have already led to climate change.

ACCORDING TO RESEARCHER GARY SHAFFER OF THE UNIVERSITY OF COPENHAGEN, THE ONLY WAY TO STOP OCEAN DEAD ZONES FROM DEVELOPING IS TO REDUCE FOSSIL FUEL EMISSIONS OVER THE NEXT SEVERAL GENERATIONS.

The burning of fossil fuels affects the oceans in another way. As more carbon dioxide enters the atmosphere, more of it dissolves into the oceans. There it undergoes chemical changes, lowering pH (which stands for potential hydrogen), or making the water more acidic. Scientists use a scale of 0 to 14 to measure pH. A pH of 7 is neutral (the amount of acids and bases are equal). The normal pH of ocean water is 8.2, or slightly basic. Atmospheric changes caused by the burning of fossil fuels are lowering this number. Seawater is still basic, but significantly less so than before. Sea organisms require a specific and constant pH to stay healthy, so even slight changes have a negative impact.

A recent study by Christopher Gobler and colleagues at Stony Brook University in New York shows that the combination of low oxygen and low pH is particularly damaging to sea life. In experiments with young bay scallops and hard clams (both economically important to fishers), the researchers found that these two factors combined to cause slower growth and higher death rates than either factor alone. Gobler thinks future studies on dead zones should focus on this combination. "Low oxygen zones in coastal and open ocean ecosystems have expanded in recent decades, a trend that will accelerate with climatic warming," he says. "There is growing recognition that low oxygen regions of the ocean are also acidified, a condition that will intensify with rising levels of atmospheric CO_2 [carbon dioxide]. . . . Hence, the low oxygen, low pH conditions used in this study will be increasingly common in the world's oceans in the future."

5 SUCCESS AND FAILURE

According to Swedish environmentalist Inger Näslund, "As with all marine issues you do not see what is down there and sea bottoms are mostly neglected because in general people think there is no life [there]. The effects of human behavior [are] many times reflected at the sea bottom and should be discussed with a louder voice."

Näslund's words are especially relevant because people can take action to reverse dead zones. The zones can recover and become healthy ecosystems. The most notable recovery occurred in the Black Sea. In the 1970s and 1980s, fertilizer runoff from fields in Russia and Ukraine turned the upper layers of the sea into a cultural dead zone. The sea suffered a complete ecosystem collapse. Between 1973 and 1990, 60 million tons (54 million metric tons) of bottom animals, including 5 million tons (4.5 million metric tons) of fish, died in the sea. Romania and Bulgaria, which also border the sea, saw a tenfold decline in the number of fish caught. The fishery industry lost an estimated $2 billion, and the tourist industry lost another $500 million annually. The region also suffered health impacts among its human population, including twenty-one thousand cases of serious waterborne diseases per year.

But by 2007, the Black Sea dead zone had largely disappeared. This reversal was spectacular although not entirely intentional. It

---

GEOENGINEERING: A QUICK FIX?

The world's largest dead zone, in the Baltic Sea, is approximately 1.5 times the size of Denmark. Efforts by surrounding countries to decrease the flow of human and industrial waste into the sea have so far failed. These projects have included managing nutrients more efficiently, reducing emissions from ships and port facilities, and improving the handling of contaminated sediments. Some scientists in Sweden are considering another solution—geoengineering. They want to build one hundred pumping stations around the sea to pump oxygen-rich surface water to the bottom. The pumps would be driven by wind turbines that harness the power of the regional winds. Some scientists say this plan would eliminate the sea's loss of oxygen and the dead zone too.

But not all scientists like the idea. Professor Daniel Conley of Sweden's Lund University considers such geoengineering projects to be "dangerous quick-fixes," which might do more harm than good. He points out that the oxygen pumps could interfere with fish reproduction, release contaminants buried in sediments, raise water temperatures, and stimulate algal blooms. "It could completely change the ecology of the Sea," Conley says. Also, the project would cost millions of dollars over decades. It would be much better, Conley says, to use the time and money to reduce land-based sources of nutrient runoff.

It is always tempting to rely on expensive technological fixes, as the Swedish scientists are advising. But such fixes often treat symptoms and avoid remedying the underlying problem, which in this case is excess nutrient runoff.

was primarily a by-product of an economic collapse in the early 1990s, when the Soviet Union broke up into independent republics. Economic hardship, combined with a rise in fertilizer costs, led farmers around the region to dramatically reduce their fertilizer use. Surrounding countries also curbed nutrient pollution with financial help from the World Bank, an international lending organization. Over the fifteen years between 1992 and 2007, nitrogen emissions into the Black Sea decreased by 20 percent and phosphorus emissions decreased by almost 50 percent. As a result, many marine populations recovered and the sea came back to life.

A partial dead-zone reversal occurred in the North Sea in northern Europe between 1985 and 2000, when nitrogen levels were reduced by 37 percent. This improvement was intentional. Countries along the Rhine River, which drains into the North Sea, took steps to decrease the amounts of sewage and industrial pollution released into the river. Other recovered dead zones include Boston Harbor in Massachusetts and Mersey Estuary on the west coast of England.

DECREASING NUTRIENT RUNOFF

The primary way to bring dead zones back to life is to reduce the amount of nutrients running off farmers' fields and into bodies of water. This involves changes in farming practices.

Best farming practices minimize the amount of fertilizer that runs off into rivers, lakes, and gulfs. Applying fertilizer in spring rather than fall can help accomplish this goal. If fertilizer is applied in the fall, it has more time to run off during rains or snows, which often results in the need for additional applications. In some cases, spring fertilizer application has decreased fertilizer runoff by 30 percent.

New technologies can also minimize nutrient runoff. Arcadia Biosciences, a company based in California, is genetically engineering crops so that their roots absorb more nitrogen. In genetic engineering, genes from two or more plants are combined to make a new plant with different, sometimes better,

To reduce runoff, farmers can apply fertilizer only as needed using systems such as this Yara N-Sensor. Mounted on a tractor, the sensor determines how much nitrogen crops are taking in and calculates the amount of fertilizer needed on each part of a field.

characteristics. In this case, the more efficient a plant is at taking up nitrogen, the less fertilizer a farmer will need to apply to the crops. In field tests, Arcadia's crops produce the same yield with only half the fertilizer used by conventional crops. Arcadia is currently working with the seed company DuPont Pioneer to produce corn seed using this technology.

In another approach, farmers can use global positioning systems (GPS) to determine the exact amount of fertilizer needed on each part of a field. A GPS satellite can precisely locate which areas of the farm field have poor crop growth and relay these locations to the farmer, who can then apply fertilizer only to those areas. This process is called precision agriculture. Because no excess fertilizer is used, runoff is minimized. A low-tech method of reducing runoff involves burying biofilters in fields to absorb excess nutrients, rather than allowing them to drain away via tiling systems. Biofilters are made of wood chips and are relatively inexpensive.

Farmers can also reduce runoff through crop rotation. For example, a farmer might alternate corn (which requires high levels of nitrogen) with soybeans (which trap nitrogen from the air and replenish soil nitrogen). Many farmers plant cover crops in the fall. The farmers don't sell these crops. Instead, they leave them on the fields all winter. This practice keeps vegetation on the land throughout the year. The additional plants increase the amount of organic matter in the soil, helping it absorb more water. The more absorbent the soil, the less water—and nutrients—will run off. In spring farmers either plow the cover crops under or leave them intact, with seeds of cash crops injected among them. Buffer strips—land with grass, trees, and shrubs, planted between strips of crop plants—help prevent erosion in the same way.

One of the most effective methods for reducing nutrient and soil runoff is no-till farming—that is, choosing not to plow fields. Instead, farmers leave the stubble and roots from the previous year's crop in the field, plant seeds through the stubble using seed drills, and inject fertilizer into the soil rather than spraying it onto the surface. This no-till process reduces phosphorus runoff by about 40 percent, cuts release of atmospheric nitrogen in half, and decreases erosion by as much as 98 percent.

ONE OF THE MOST EFFECTIVE METHODS FOR REDUCING NUTRIENT AND SOIL RUNOFF IS NO-TILL FARMING—THAT IS, CHOOSING NOT TO PLOW FIELDS.

In the past twenty-five years, about 36 percent of US cropland has been converted to no-till fields. US farmers often choose no-till agriculture for economic reasons, because it prevents erosion and decreases the amount of fertilizer and fossil fuels needed. If done extensively and over a long time period, these decreases in fertilizer and fossil fuel use would also contribute to the control of global warming. But US adoption of no-till farming is slow, partly because the initial investment for no-till drills and other equipment is so

An agricultural specialist inspects a no-till cotton crop at a farm in Arkansas. New cotton plants grow amid the stubble and roots of the previous season's crop. The system cuts down on erosion, since farmers don't use plows to dig up roots or to plant new seeds. And the extra organic matter helps the soil retain water.

large. While no-till farming helps retain water, it may also increase the likelihood of fungal diseases. Also, no-till farming has one major disadvantage. Weed control is done with pesticides in both plowed and no-till fields. But since plowing helps control weeds, often more pesticides are required to control them in no-till fields. This means the runoff that does occur will contain both fertilizers and toxic pesticides. Finally, although no-till eventually leads to larger harvests, this increase may take a decade or more.

Better irrigation practices are also essential to conserving nutrients. Most irrigation systems apply water to the surface of the soil, either by sprinkler systems or by flooding the entire field or individual rows. Much of this water runs off the surface rather than soaking into the soil, and it takes many soil nutrients with it. With sprinkler systems, additional water is lost through evaporation before it even reaches the soil surface. Drip irrigation is much more efficient. It controls the flow of water and delivers water directly to the top of the soil or slightly beneath it, at a much slower rate. This decreases erosion and runoff. However, very few US farmers use drip irrigation because of its high cost. Even though farmers would save water and money in the long run, many cannot afford or do not want to make the large initial investment for new equipment.

According to Rebecca Flood, assistant commissioner for the Minnesota Pollution Control Agency, if farmers use the most efficient techniques, they can decrease nitrogen pollution by 19 percent. She estimates that increasing efficiency of fertilizer use on 13.2 million acres (5.34 million hectares) will reduce nitrogen loss by 13 percent. Planting cover crops on 800,000 acres (323,750 hectares) will reduce it another 3 percent. Nitrogen retained in soil and crops will not run off into rivers and therefore will not contribute to the Gulf of Mexico dead zone.

With drip irrigation, farmers provide water to plants at ground level. The water immediately soaks into the soil, with little lost to runoff or evaporation. Sprinklers and other irrigation devices can be much more wasteful.

RESTORING WETLANDS

In a natural ecosystem, without human interference, excess nutrients are removed from water naturally. For instance, during floods, rivers deposit nutrient-rich sediment onto their floodplains— the land around a river that may be submerged during a flood. The sediment dries out and becomes soil. The rivers continue on to their final destinations carrying cleaner water. The soil and plant roots of wetlands also trap excess nutrients.

Over the centuries, Americans have drained and filled millions of acres of wetlands to create farmland or roads, homes, and other buildings. By 2015 only about 100 million acres (40 million hectares) of the nation's original 220 million (89 million hectares) remain. These wetlands are disappearing at a rate of about 60,000 acres (24,280 hectares) per year. With the loss of wetlands, US river ecosystems are much less able to trap nutrients before they reach the sea. This contributes to the creation of dead zones.

Restoring wetlands, therefore, is a major way to reduce nutrient input into rivers such as the Mississippi. Restoration requires teams of people trained in hydrology (the study of Earth's water distribution and circulation), ecology, engineering, and environmental planning. It also requires community involvement. In one approach, known as passive restoration, people remove the threats to a wetland and let nature go to work. For example, if cattle are being grazed in a wetland area, farmers move them somewhere else, allowing the wetland plants to grow without interference. This approach works if wetland plants, animals, and soil types are still present in the area. If they aren't, people can use active methods of restoration. These include recontouring, or reshaping, the land, changing the direction of water flow, and planting and seeding the area with wetland plants. To recontour the land, workers use bulldozers to move soil. For example, soil may be removed to form a depression, allowing more water to drain into the area and make it more like a marsh. Workers can also place culverts (large pipes) or low dams to change the direction of water flow as needed.

TAKING BACK THE GULF

The US government runs a number of programs aimed at improving the health of land and waterways in the United States. For instance, the Conservation Reserve Program encourages farmers to let certain lands rest, allowing native plants and animal species to return there. The USDA, EPA, and other US agencies run programs aimed at improving water quality in US lakes and rivers. These programs, although not specifically designed to reduce dead zones, can help with that goal by reducing fertilizer use and the amount of nutrients entering US waterways.

Some programs are designed specifically to reduce the Gulf dead zone. For example, in 1997 the EPA established the Mississippi River/ Gulf of Mexico Watershed Nutrient Task Force. In 2001 the task force introduced a $15 billion action plan designed to reduce hypoxia in the Gulf. The original plan was to cut the size of the yearly dead zone in half, to approximately 1,900 square miles (4,921 sq. km), and to reduce the amount of nitrogen received from the Mississippi River by 30 percent by 2015. The task force set out to accomplish this by reducing pollution from farms and urban areas. It encouraged farmers to use less fertilizer and to restore natural buffer strips along streams. A 2013 assessment showed that the original 2001 goal was far from being met. The yearly average dead zone measured approximately 5,100 square miles (13,209 sq. km)—2.7 times higher than the goal—and amounts of nitrogen and phosphorus entering the Gulf had increased.

To fight HABs, in 1998 Congress passed the Harmful Algal Bloom and Hypoxia Research and Control Act. The act was revised and amended in December 2004. The law empowers NOAA to study HABs and to develop plans to prevent and control them. NOAA has even developed a system to give people advance warning before HABs form. They can then buy bottled water, avoid seafood and boat travel in the area, and remain out of the water until the HAB is gone. The Harmful Algal Blooms Observing System combines algal cell counts and environmental information into a single interactive map that gives scientists, environmental managers, and others up-to-date information about HABs around the Gulf of Mexico. The Harmful Algal Bloom Operational Forecast System provides daily reports on the concentration of *Karenia brevis*, the red tide organism, along the coasts of Florida and Texas.

CHESAPEAKE BAY CLEANUP

Some restoration efforts have involved private organizations as well as the government. For instance, the Chesapeake Bay Foundation, founded in 1967, has been involved in trying to reduce the Chesapeake Bay dead zone. Working with the EPA and state governments, the foundation began a bay cleanup effort in 1983. It focused on decreasing the influx of nitrogen and phosphorus pollution into the bay.

As part of the cleanup, cities near the bay have upgraded their sewer and storm water systems. Farmers have created fertilizer

The Chesapeake Bay Foundation (CBF) works to keep the bay healthy with the involvement of community groups, students, and other volunteers. These high school students inspect organisms from the Shenandoah River, which drains into the bay, in a CBF program designed to monitor life in the river.

management plans and planted cover crops. The federal government has made businesses near the bay adhere to the Clean Air Act. This law requires factories, power plants, and other groups to limit the amount of pollution they put into the air.

Some progress has been made. In 2011 a team from Johns Hopkins University in Baltimore, Maryland, worked with ecologist Michael Kemp to study the extent of the bay's dead zone throughout the summer. They discovered that the dead zone was as extensive in early summer as it had been in the 1980s. But from mid-July on, it was smaller than it was in the 1980s. It also lasted for less time—110 days, rather than 130 days. Between 1987 and 2012, nutrient levels in the bay had decreased by about 20 percent. Lowered nutrient levels have resulted in a fourfold regrowth of grasses in some, but not all, parts of the bay. Scientists hope that these improvements will lead to others.

WHY ISN'T IT WORKING?

Despite some successes, cleaning up dead zones is difficult. One problem is that different branches of government are sometimes working toward different goals. For example, the EPA works to increase corn production to meet US ethanol goals. But increased corn production increases nitrogen pollution. At the same time, the EPA runs groups such as the Mississippi River/Gulf of Mexico Watershed Nutrient Task Force to limit nitrogen pollution. In this case, the push to grow more corn for fuel appears to be stronger than the push to use less nitrogen. For this reason, the success of projects to improve the hypoxia situation in the Gulf of Mexico has been limited.

Another complication is that agricultural runoff can originate more than 1,000 miles (1,609 km) away from the actual dead zone. For example, the decisions of farmers in Minnesota and Iowa can impact the growth of the Gulf dead zone. Yet they rarely think about the dead zone problems of shrimpers, fishers, or oyster farmers in Louisiana. Shrimper Darren Martin quotes an old saying: "Everything good comes down the Mississippi—and so does everything bad."

In addition, government can only do so much to fight against nitrogen and phosphorus pollution. The federal government does not have the power to regulate chemical fertilizers—the major source of nitrogen. And regulation through the federal Clean Water Act, passed in 1972, is only partially helpful. The law applies only to point source pollution—that is, pollution coming from a single source, such as a factory or sewage plant. Yet nonpoint source pollution—which comes from many sources, including agricultural fields, city streets, and lawns—is mostly responsible for creating dead zones. The EPA recommends ways to limit agricultural nonpoint source pollution, but it does not regulate it because, by definition, it cannot precisely identify the sources of nonpoint source pollution. Therefore no one can be held accountable.

> "EVERYTHING GOOD COMES DOWN THE MISSISSIPPI—AND SO DOES EVERYTHING BAD."
>
> AN OLD SAYING QUOTED BY SHRIMPER DARREN MARTIN

Many cleanup programs in the United States are voluntary. That is, government agencies encourage but do not require farmers, cities, and businesses to reduce the amount of pollution entering bodies of water. In some cases, farmers and others are paid to make changes. But the evidence shows that voluntary programs, even those backed by billions of dollars in federal money, have not effectively decreased runoff.

Decreasing or eliminating Gulf dead zones will not be cheap. For instance, to minimize manure runoff, farmers can use systems called methane digesters. A digester holds manure in airtight tanks and heats it to form methane gas. The methane is then used as a fuel to provide energy either on or off the farm. Most small farmers cannot afford methane digesters. Many large businesses, such as fertilizer companies and the industrial farms known as agribusinesses, are much more concerned with making money than with restoring ecosystems. They support using more fertilizer, not less. In fact, the fertilizer industry is booming in farm states. Illinois governor Pat Quinn, in 2014, approved construction of a huge new fertilizer plant run by Cronus Fertilizers in Tuscola, Illinois. Quinn touted the boon to farmers and the jobs that would be created for Illinois. Similarly, Iowa governor Terry Branstad opposes stricter regulations on chemical fertilizers, which might cut into farm and fertilizer business profits.

Big businesses and their political allies in farm states exert tremendous influence on members of Congress, other politicians, and agencies like the EPA. Environmental groups such as the National Resources Defense Council (NRDC) want to see the federal government stand up to big corporations. NRDC senior attorney Ann Alexander says, "For too long, EPA has stood on the sidelines while our nation's waters slowly choke on algae." She believes the EPA has failed to set standards and establish cleanup plans for nitrogen and phosphorus pollution because of strong pressure from agribusiness industries not to act.

In the end, specific human efforts to clean up dead zones might be less powerful than the natural forces of weather and climate. For example, rainfall has a strong effect on grass recovery in the Chesapeake Bay. During dry years, when less sediment enters the bay, water clarity is greater and more grasses grow. Conversely, during wet years, more sediment washes into the bay, decreasing water clarity and harming grass recovery. Efforts to control human effects on climate change—for example, lowering fossil fuel emissions—may be much more effective in the long run than voluntary nutrient cleanup programs.

WHAT LIES AHEAD?

Scientists tell us that if the problem of dead zones is not addressed, it will intensify in the coming years. The combined impacts of excess nutrients, global warming, oil spills, and other environmental stresses will ensure that dead zones around the world become

larger and last longer. Marine species, food sources for humans and animals, and local economies face the risk of total devastation. However, the general public and most politicians do not see the urgent need to tackle the problem.

All of Earth's ecosystems are interconnected. The first freshwater that enters the Mississippi in northern Minnesota ultimately affects life in the Gulf of Mexico, and it affects every other ecosystem along the way. Humans are a vital part of these interconnecting ecosystems. Some ecosystems—croplands, for example—are almost entirely human-made. People plant them, care for them, harvest them, and eat the food or use the energy sources they produce. Other ecosystems may appear natural but are profoundly affected by people. When we cut trees and grasses, drain and fill in wetlands, release pollutants into rivers and lakes, and burn fossil fuels that stimulate global warming, we are affecting all ecosystems and organisms, including our own species. Currently, the world's dead zones are growing. They will decline only if people recognize their role in the interconnections among ecosystems and take action.

SOURCE NOTES

4–5 Perry Beeman Gannett, "Dead Zone: Runoff from Midwest Farms Plagues Gulf," Louisiana Universities Marine Consortium, November 3, 2012, http://www .gulfhypoxia.net/News/default.asp?XMLFilename=201211151505.xml.

7 "The Gulf of Mexico Dead Zone," Science Museum of Minnesota, accessed July 11, 2014, http://www.smm.org/deadzone/top.html.

8 News editor, "Dead Zone Affects Fisheries in the Northern Gulf of Mexico," Louisiana Seafood News, accessed July 7, 2014, http://www.louisianaseafoodnews .com/2011/11/02/dead-zone-affects-fisheries-in-the-northern-gulf-of-mexico/.

8 Alex Hannaford, "Life in the Dead Zone," Texas Observer, January 27, 2014, http:// www.texasobserver.org/life-dead-zone/.

8 Virginia Institute of Marine Science, "Study Shows Continued Spread of 'Dead Zones'; Lack of Oxygen Now a Key Stressor on Marine Ecosystems," ScienceDaily, August 15, 2008, http://www.sciencedaily.com /releases/2008/08/080814154325.htm.

9 David Biello, "Oceanic Dead Zones Continue to Spread," Scientific American, August 15, 2008, http://www.scientificamerican.com/article/oceanic-dead -zones-spread/.

10 Virginia Institute of Marine Science, "Study Shows Continued Spread of 'Dead Zones.'"

22 Lisa A. Levin, "Deep-Ocean Life Where Oxygen Is Scarce," American Scientist 90 (September–October 2002): 436–444, http://levin.ucsd.edu/research/Am Sci 2002.pdf.

26 Lauren Mills, "Sending It on Downriver: Iowan Nutrients in the Dead Zone," Iowa Center for Public Affairs Journalism, April 1, 2012, http://iowawatch .org/2012/04/01/sending-it-on-downriver-iowan-nutrients-in-the-dead-zone/#.

32 Gannett, "Dead Zone."

37 Jonathan Foley, "It's Time to Rethink America's Corn System," Scientific American, March 5, 2013, http://www.scientificamerican.com/article/time-to -rethink-corn/.

38 Biello, "Oceanic Dead Zones."

38 "Science Focus: Dead Zones. Creeping Dead Zones," GES DISC, last modified June 21, 2012, http://disc.sci.gsfc.nasa.gov/education-and-outreach/additional /science-focus/ocean-color/science_focus.shtml/dead_zones.shtml.

42   Brad Plumer, "A Toxic Algae Scare Has Left 500,000 People in Ohio without Drinking Water," *Vox*, last modified August 3, 2014, http://www.vox .com/2014/8/3/5963645/a-toxic-algae-bloom-has-left-400000-people-in-ohio -without-drinking.

46   Amy Simmons, "Scientists Fear Mass Extinction as Oceans Choke," *ABC News*, last modified November 30, 2010, http://www.abc.net.au/news/2010 -11-30/scientists-fear-mass-extinction-as-oceans-choke/2357322.

47   Jessica Marshall, "Dead Zone in Gulf Linked to Oil," *Discovery*, July 9, 2010, http://news.discovery.com/earth/weather-extreme-events/gulf-mexico -dead-zone-oil-spill.htm.

49   Ibid.

50   Dahr Jamail, "Gulf Seafood Deformities Alarm Scientists," *Aljazeera*, April 20, 2012, http://www.aljazeera.com/indepth/features/2012/04 /201241682318260912.html.

50   Ibid.

50   Ibid.

53   Stony Brook University, "Ocean Dead Zones More Deadly for Marine Life Than Previously Predicted," *ScienceDaily*, January 9, 2014, http://www .sciencedaily.com/releases/2014/01/140109003752.htm.

54   Tom Levitt, "Can Oxygen Pump Breathe Life into Ocean 'Dead Zone'?," *CNN*, last modified July 17, 2012, http://www.cnn.com/2012/07/17/world/europe /dead-zone-baltic-oxygen/.

55   Levitt, "Oxygen Pump."

64–65   Gannett, "Dead Zone."

66   Josh Mogerman, "Dead Zone Decision: Court Ruling Forces EPA Action on Mississippi River Pollution," National Resources Defense Council, September 23, 2013, http://www.nrdc.org/media/2013/130923a.asp.

GLOSSARY

acidic: having a pH (a measure of the concentration of hydrogen ions in a solution) less than 7 on the pH scale of 0 to 14. The lower the pH on the scale, the stronger the acid. In chemistry, acids release hydrogen ions when dissolved and react with bases (compounds that have a pH greater than 7) to form salts.

algal bloom: a very rapid explosion of growth in an algal population; also called a phytoplankton bloom

anaerobic: not requiring oxygen for respiration

best farming practice: for fertilizer use, applying just enough fertilizer for crops to grow while at the same time limiting the amount that will be lost in runoff

climate change: a measurable change in global climate patterns, including changes in temperature, rainfall, and storms, lasting over a period of thirty years or more. Scientists point to the burning of fossil fuels, which releases greenhouse gases into the atmosphere, as responsible for the rapid climate change since the late twentieth century.

cyanobacteria: a type of photosynthesizing blue-green bacteria that commonly cause algal blooms and hypoxia in bodies of freshwater

dead zone: a region of a body of water where the oxygen content is zero or very low; also called a hypoxic zone

delta: a land-form, usually V-shaped, that forms at the mouth of a large river as the force of flowing water deposits silt and sediment from the river there

distributary: a river branching off from a main river and entering a delta separately. The Atchafalaya River is a distributary of the Mississippi. They both enter the Mississippi River delta.

ecosystem: a biological system consisting of all organisms in a geographical area, the nonliving environment, and all interactions occurring among them. Examples of ecosystems include ponds, forests, and farm fields.

erosion: the natural process of removal of the top layers of soil from a landscape by the action of wind or water

estuary: a coastal body of water where freshwater from rivers and streams flows into the ocean and mixes with seawater

ethanol: a type of alcohol used in alcoholic beverages and also burned as a fuel. Ethanol can be produced from certain plants, such as corn.

eutrophication: the process by which a water body receives excess nutrients, usually nitrogen and phosphorus

fertilizer: a chemical nutrient required for plant growth. Farmers often add fertilizers to the soil to supply or replenish nutrients lost by erosion or the harvesting of crops.

floodplain: the flat area on either side of a river, into which water flows during floods. Nutrient-containing sediment from the river is deposited on the floodplain.

fossil fuels: petroleum products (coal, oil, and natural gas) made from the remains of ancient plants and animals. These products are formed naturally underground over millions of years by the forces of heat and pressure.

genetic engineering: a biological practice in which scientists combine genes from two or more organisms to make a new, different organism

harmful algal bloom (HAB): an algal or cyanobacterium bloom that contains a toxin and causes death or illness in organisms. It also causes hypoxia in the water.

hypoxia: oxygen depletion in a body of water. Water is hypoxic when its oxygen concentration is 2 parts per million or less.

nonpoint source pollution: pollution entering a water body from multiple sources. Runoff from agricultural fields is an example of nonpoint source pollution.

organic matter: matter composed of the remains of living organisms and their waste products. An important component of soil and sediment, organic matter is eaten (broken down) by bacteria and other decomposers.

photosynthesis: the process by which green plants and algae (phytoplankton) make their own food using energy from the sun and carbon dioxide from the air or water. Photosynthesis produces oxygen as a by-product.

phytoplankton: tiny, single-celled algae that form the base of the food web in oceans, lakes, and estuaries

point source pollution: pollution entering a water body from a single source, such as a power plant or sewage plant

respiration: a series of chemical reactions by which all living organisms break down food to release energy and carry out their life processes. Respiration can be either aerobic (requiring oxygen) or anaerobic (using compounds other than oxygen).

salinity: salt content, or the percentage of salt in a water body. For example, freshwater has a salinity near zero, while ocean salinity is approximately 3.5 percent.

stratification: when water in a lake or bay separates into layers of different density, due to differences in temperature or salinity

tributary: a river or stream flowing into a larger river or lake. The Missouri River is a tributary of the Mississippi, for instance.

watershed: the land area drained by a river

wetlands: waterlogged areas of land, such as marshes and swamps. Wetlands trap nutrients and lessen the effects of floods on the landscape.

SELECTED BIBLIOGRAPHY

Atkin, Emily. "In One Month, the Chesapeake Bay's 'Most Critical' Pollution Issue Could Be Unsolvable." *ClimateProgress*, August 8, 2014. http://thinkprogress.org/climate/2014/08/08/3467685/chesapeake-bay-pollution-conowingo-dam/.

Biello, David. "Fertilizer Runoff Overwhelms Streams and Rivers—Creating Vast 'Dead Zones.'" *Scientific American*, March 14, 2008. http://www.scientificamerican.com/article/fertilizer-runoff-overwhelms-streams/.

———. "How Will the Oil Spill Impact the Gulf's Dead Zone?" *Scientific American*, June 3, 2010. http://www.scientificamerican.com/article/how-will-the-oil-spill-impact-dead-zone/.

———. "Oceanic Dead Zones Continue to Spread." *Scientific American*, August 15, 2008. http://www.scientificamerican.com/article/oceanic-dead-zones-spread/.

"Cleaning Up Ecological 'Dead Zones.'" GW Planet Forward, November 21, 2012. http://www.planetforward.org/tv-segments/cleaning-up-ecological-dead-zones.

"The Conowingo Dam and Chesapeake Bay." Chesapeake Bay Foundation. Accessed April 1, 2015. http://www.cbf.org/about-the-bay/issues/polluted-runoff/conowingo-dam-and-chesapeake-bay.

Dybas, Cheryl Lyn. "Dead Zones Spreading in World Oceans." *BioScience* 55, no. 7 (July 2005): 552–557. http://bioscience.oxfordjournals.org/content/55/7/552.full.pdf+html.

"The Energy-Water Collision: Corn Ethanol's Threat to Water Resources." Union of Concerned Scientists. Accessed April 1, 2015. http://www.ucsusa.org/assets/documents/clean_energy/ew3/corn-ethanol-and-water-quality.pdf.

"Environmental Solutions: Chesapeake Bay." American Farmland Trust. Accessed April 1, 2015. http://162.242.222.244/programs/environment/solutions/chesapeake-bay.asp

"The Facts about Nutrient Pollution." Environmental Protection Agency. Accessed April 1, 2015. http://midwestadvocates.org/assets/resources/nutrient_pollution_factsheet.pdf.

Fargione, Joe. "How to Kill the Gulf's Dead-Zone Zombie." *Grist*, August 10, 2011. http://grist.org/pollution/2011-08-10-how-to-kill-the-gulfs-dead-zone-zombie/.

Fincham, Michael W. "The Bay-Grass Surprise." *Chesapeake Quarterly*, December 2012. http://www.chesapeakequarterly.net/V11N4/main1/.

———."A Chesapeake Bay Recovery: Half Empty or Half Full?" *Chesapeake Quarterly*, December 2012. http://www.chesapeakequarterly.net/V11N4/intro/.

"Fisheries in the Dead Zone." NOAA Fisheries, July 29, 2013. http://www.fisheries.noaa.gov/stories/2013/07/7_26_13mapping_the_dead_zone.html.

Foley, Jonathan. "It's Time to Rethink America's Corn System." *Scientific American*, March 5, 2013. http://www.scientificamerican.com/article/time-to-rethink-corn/.

"From Farmer to Shrimper: The Dead Zone." Minnesota Department of Natural Resources, Division of Ecological Services. Accessed July 7, 2014. http://files .dnr.state.mn.us/assistance/backyard/healthyrivers/course/300/305_00.htm.

Gannett, Perry Beeman. "Dead Zone: Runoff from Midwest Farms Plagues Gulf." Louisiana Universities Marine Consortium, November 3, 2012. http://www .gulfhypoxia.net/News/default.asp?XMLFilename=201211151505.xml.

Goldenberg, Suzanne. "Biologists Find 'Dead Zones' around BP Oil Spill in Gulf." *Guardian* (Manchester), June 30, 2010. http://www.theguardian.com /environment/2010/jun/30/biologists-find-oil-spill-deadzones.

Gulick, Amy. "No Oxygen, No Life: The Gulf of Mexico's 'Dead Zone.'" *Dive Training.* Accessed July 30, 2014. http://dtmag.com/Stories/Ocean%20Science/12-03 -ecoseas.htm.

Hannaford, Alex. "Life in the Dead Zone." *Texas Observer*, January 27, 2014. http:// www.texasobserver.org/life-dead-zone/.

"Harmful Algal Blooms." National Oceanic and Atmospheric Administration. Last modified August 11, 2014. http://oceanservice.noaa.gov/hazards/hab/.

Henry, Tom. "Algae-Produced Microcystin May Follow Blooms across Lake." *Toledo Blade*, August 21, 2014. http://www.toledoblade.com/local/2014/08/21/Algae -produced-microcystin-may-follow-blooms-across-lake.print.

Hirsch, Jesse. "No-Till Farming: What's the Deal?" *Modern Farmer,* August 30, 2013. http://modernfarmer.com/2013/08/7-facts-till-farming/.

Horowitz, John, Robert Ebel, and Kohei Ueda. "'No-Till' Farming Is a Growing Practice." USDA. Economic Information Bulletin No. 70. November 2010. Accessed March 22, 2015. http://www.ers.usda.gov/publications/eib-economic -information-bulletin/eib70.aspx.

"Hypoxia in the Gulf of Mexico and Long Island Sound." Environmental Protection Agency. Last modified June 2, 2011. http://cfpub.epa.gov/eroe/index .cfm?fuseaction=detail.viewInd&lv=list.listByAlpha&r=235290&subtop=274.

"Hypoxia 101." Environmental Protection Agency, Office of Oceans, Wetlands, and Watersheds. Accessed July 27, 2014. http://water.epa.gov/type/watersheds/ named/msbasin/hypoxia101.cfm.

"Issue Brief: Ocean Hypoxia–'Dead Zones.'" United Nations Development Programme, May 15, 2013. http://www.undp.org/content/undp/en /home/librarypage/environment-energy/water_governance/ocean_and _coastalareagovernance/issue-brief---ocean-hypoxia--dead-zones-/.

Jacobsen, Rowan. "Saving the Seas: Reducing Fertilizer Runoff to Resurrect Ocean Dead Zones." *Popular Science*, May 6, 2011. http://www.popsci.com/science /article/2011-04/reducing-fertilizer-runoff-resurrect-ocean-dead-zones.

Jamail, Dahr. "Gulf Seafood Deformities Alarm Scientists." *Aljazeera*, April 20, 2012. http://www.aljazeera.com/indepth/features/2012/04/201241682318260912 .html.

Kozacek, Codi. "World Stands By as Algae and Dead Zones Ruin Water." Circle of Blue, September 25, 2014. http://www.circleofblue.org/waternews/2014/world /draft-world-stands-algae-dead-zones-ruin-water/.

"Large Dead Zone Growing in Gulf of Mexico." Texas A&M University, June 27, 2013. http://today.tamu.edu/2013/06/27/large-dead-zone-growing-in-gulf-of-mexico/

Levin, Lisa A. "Deep-Ocean Life Where Oxygen Is Scarce." American Scientist 90 (September–October 2002): 436–444. http://levin.ucsd.edu/research/Am%20 Sci%202002.pdf.

Levitt, Tom. "Can Oxygen Pump Breathe Life into Ocean 'Dead Zone'?" CNN. Last modified July 17, 2012. http://www.cnn.com/2012/07/17/world/europe/dead-zone-baltic-oxygen/.

Marshall, Jessica. "Dead Zone in Gulf Linked to Oil." Discovery, July 9, 2010. http:// news.discovery.com/earth/weather-extreme-events/gulf-mexico-dead-zone -oil-spill.htm.

Mazza, Ed. "Dead Fish Fill Marina Del Rey, Creating Major Stink for SoCal Harbor." Huffington Post, May 19, 2014. http://www.huffingtonpost.com/2014/05/19/dead -fish-marina-del-rey_n_5349962.html.

Mills, Lauren. "Sending It on Downriver: Iowan Nutrients in the Dead Zone." Iowa Center for Public Affairs Journalism, April 1, 2012. http://iowawatch .org/2012/04/01/sending-it-on-downriver-iowan-nutrients-in-the-dead-zone/#.

———. "The Story of Nitrogen: A Trip Down the Mississippi." Iowa Center for Public Affairs Journalism, March 31, 2012. http://iowawatch.org/2012/03/31/the-story -of-nitrogen-a-trip-down-the-mississippi/.

Nassauer, Joan Iverson, Mary V. Santelmann, and Donald Scavia, eds. From the Corn Belt to the Gulf: Societal and Environmental Implications of Alternative Agriculture Futures. Washington, DC: Resources for the Future, 2007.

"Nitrogen and Phosphorus." Chesapeake Bay Foundation. Accessed April 1, 2015. http://www.cbf.org/about-the-bay/issues/dead-zones/nitrogen-phosphorus.

"Nitrogen Use Efficiency." Agricultural Sustainability Institute at UCDavis. Accessed April 1, 2015. http://asi.ucdavis.edu/research/nitrogen/n-science/nitrogen-use -efficiency.

Ostrom, Nathaniel E. "The Dead Zone: The Deepwater Horizon Oil Spill versus the Dead Zone in the Northern Gulf of Mexico—Which Is Worse?" Prairie Fire, September 2010. http://www.prairiefirenewspaper.com/2010/09/the-dead-zone.

"Overview of Hypoxia and Nutrient Pollution." National Center for Coastal Ocean Science. Last modified February 16, 2011. http://www.cop.noaa.gov/stressors /pollution/.

Philpott, Tom. "Why This Year's Gulf Dead Zone Is Twice as Big as Last Year's." Mother Jones, August 14, 2013. http://www.motherjones.com/tom -philpott/2013/08/gulf-of-mexico-dead-zone-growth.

Plumer, Brad. "A Toxic Algae Scare Has Left 500,000 People in Ohio without Drinking Water." *Vox*. Last modified August 3, 2014. http://www.vox.com/2014/8/3/5963645/a-toxic-algae-bloom-has-left-400000-people-in-ohio-without-drinking.

———. "No-Till Farming Is on the Rise. That's Actually a Big Deal." *Washington Post*, November 9, 2013. http://www.washingtonpost.com/blogs/wonkblog/wp/2013/11/09/no-till-farming-is-on-the-rise-thats-actually-a-big-deal/.

Reader, Ruth. "The Biggest Dead Zones in America's Waterways." *Motherboard*, July 2, 2013. http://motherboard.vice.com/blog/the-biggest-dead-zones-in-americas-waterways.

Schindler, David W., and John R. Vallentyne. *The Algal Bowl: Overfertilization of the World's Freshwaters and Estuaries*. London: Earthscan, 2008.

Simmons, Amy. "Scientists Fear Mass Extinction as Oceans Choke." *ABC News*. Last modified November 30, 2010. http://www.abc.net.au/news/2010-11-30/scientists-fear-mass-extinction-as-oceans-choke/2357322.

Smith, Matt. "Empty Nets in Louisiana Three Years after the Spill." *CNN*, April 29, 2013. http://www.cnn.com/2013/04/27/us/gulf-disaster-fishing-industry/.

Soos, Andy. "A Very Big Dead Zone." *ENN*, June 19, 2013. http://www.enn.com/top_stories/article/46117.

Spotts, Pete. "Toledo Water Crisis May Be Over, but Toxic Algae Blooms Are in Our Future." *Christian Science Monitor*, August 4, 2014. http://www.csmonitor.com/USA/2014/0804/Toledo-water-crisis-may-be-over-but-toxic-algae-blooms-are-in-our-future-video.

Stony Brook University. "Ocean Dead Zones More Deadly for Marine Life Than Previously Predicted." *ScienceDaily*, January 9, 2014. http://www.sciencedaily.com/releases/2014/01/140109003752.htm.

Thompson, Andrea. "Future of the Ocean: Expanding Dead Zones." *LiveScience*, January 28, 2009. http://www.livescience.com/7675-future-ocean-expanding-dead-zones.html.

Virginia Institute of Marine Science. "Study Shows Continued Spread of 'Dead Zones'; Lack of Oxygen Now a Key Stressor on Marine Ecosystems." *ScienceDaily*, August 15, 2008. http://www.sciencedaily.com/releases/2008/08/080814154325.htm.

FOR FURTHER INFORMATION

BOOKS

Friedman, Lauri S., ed. *Oceans*. Farmington Hills, MI: Greenhaven, 2011.

Gay, Kathlyn. *Food: The New Gold*. Minneapolis: Twenty-First Century Books, 2013.

Gerdes, Louise, ed. *Endangered Oceans*. Farmington Hills, MI: Greenhaven, 2009.

Goldstein, Margaret. *Fuel under Fire: Petroleum and Its Perils*. Minneapolis: Twenty-First Century Books, 2016.

Hayes, Denis. *Cowed: The Hidden Impact of 93 Million Cows on America's Health, Economy, Politics, Culture, and Environment*. New York: W. W. Norton, 2015.

Heinrichs, Ann. *Maintaining Earth's Oceans*. New Rochelle, NY: Benchmark, 2011.

Jacobsen, Rowan. *Shadows on the Gulf: A Journey through Our Last Great Wetland*. New York: Bloomsbury USA, 2011.

Kallen, Stuart A. *Running Dry: The Global Water Crisis*. Minneapolis: Twenty-First Century Books, 2015.

Mitchell, Alanna. *Seasick: Ocean Change and the Extinction of Life on Earth*. Chicago: University of Chicago Press, 2012.

Roberts, Jack L. *Organic Agriculture: Protecting Our Food Supply or Chasing Imaginary Risk*. Minneapolis: Twenty-First Century Books, 2012.

WEBSITES

Bountiful Oceans
http://www.greenpeace.org/international/en/campaigns/oceans/
The international environmental group Greenpeace hosts this website about oceans, threats to ocean life, and how to keep the world's oceans healthy.

Chesapeake Bay Foundation
http://www.cbf.org
The Chesapeake Bay Foundation works to keep the bay clean. The organization's website explains how nitrogen pollution, chemical contamination, climate change, and other hazards are harming life in the bay and what can be done to protect it.

Gulf of Mexico Dead Zone
http://www.smm.org/deadzone/top.html
This website from the Science Museum of Minnesota explains in simple language the causes, formation, and effects of dead zones, accompanied by graphics and videos.

Hypoxia in the Northern Gulf of Mexico
http://www.gulfhypoxia.net/default.asp
Created by the National Oceanic and Atmospheric Administration and the Louisiana Universities Marine Consortium, this website gives general information about hypoxia, its causes, and research being carried out on the dead zone in the northern Gulf of Mexico. The site includes up-to-date news coverage and links to other informational websites.

Hypoxia 101
http://water.epa.gov/type/watersheds/named/msbasin/hypoxia101.cfm
This website from the Environmental Protection Agency includes basic information on ocean hypoxia (dead zones), with specific information on the Gulf of Mexico dead zone. It includes diagrams, a short movie, and links to further information.

Ocean Literacy Campaign
http://www.coexploration.org/oceanliteracy/documents/OceanLitChart.pdf
This online guidebook explores Earth's oceans, including ocean life, how the ocean influences weather and climate, and ways in which the oceans and human society are interconnected.

USGS Water Science School
http://water.usgs.gov/edu/
Created by the US Geological Survey, this website offers general information on the water cycle, surface water, and groundwater. The section titled "Water Quality" includes background information on nitrogen, phosphorus, and runoff.

FILMS

King Corn. DVD. Directed by Aaron Woolf, Ian Cheney, and Curt Ellis. San Francisco: Independent Television Service, 2007.
This documentary digs into the central role that corn plays in the US diet and culture. The filmmakers examine corn used in fast food, the use of fertilizer on cornfields, genetically modified corn seeds, the use of corn as animal feed, and more.

Troubled Waters: A Mississippi River Story. DVD. Directed by Larkin McPhee. Minneapolis: Bell Museum of Natural History, 2012.
This fifty-seven-minute DVD describes Mississippi River pollution caused by farming and describes the Gulf of Mexico dead zone that results. The filmmakers make the case for changing US agricultural policy to deal with this problem.

INDEX

PHOTO ACKNOWLEDGMENTS

The images in this book are used with the permission of: Lamiot/Wikimedia Commons (SA 3.0) (algae backgrounds); © Julie Dermansky/CORBIS, p. 5; © Dennis Macdonald/Getty Images, p. 6; © Ricardo Moares/CORBIS, p. 10; © Laura Westlund/ Independent Picture Service, pp. 11, 27, 29, 39; REUTERS/Jianan Yu, p. 12; © iStockphoto.com/ifish, p. 15; © George Grall/National Geographic/Getty Images, p. 18; © Scott Leslie/Minden Pictures, p. 20; Courtesy of the National Oceanic and Atmospheric Administration Central Library Photo Collection, p. 23; REUTERS/Hans Deryk/Newscom, p. 25; © Scott Sinklier/Alamy, p. 33; © imageBROKER/SuperStock, p. 35; © Bill Bachman/Science Source, p. 41; AP Photo/Haraz N. Ghanbari, p. 43; AP Photo/Imaginechina, p. 46; REUTERS/Lee Celano, p. 49; © Sergey Borisov/Alamy, p. 51; © User:bdk/Wikimedia Commons/CC-BY-SA-3.0, p. 57; © Bill Barksdale/ AgStock Images/CORBIS, p. 57; © Oxford/E+/Getty Images, p. 60; AP Photo/Daily News-Record, Nikki Fox, p. 63.

Front cover: © Jiang Kehong/Xinhua Press/CORBIS.

ABOUT THE AUTHOR

Carol Hand has a PhD in zoology with a specialization in marine ecology from the University of Georgia. Before becoming a science writer, she taught college biology, wrote for standardized testing companies, and developed multimedia science curricula. She has written more than twenty science books for young people on topics ranging from glaciers to genetics to environmental engineering. The books she considers most important are those describing nature and the environment, especially those documenting the human impact on ecosystems—how we are changing our life support systems and how we can learn to live in harmony with nature. This is her first YA title for Twenty-First Century Books.